Frances

G000141285

Africa

I want to work

in...

Africa

How to Move Your Career to the
World's Most Exciting Continent

Also by Frances Mensah Williams:
Everyday Heroes: Learning from the Careers of Successful Black
Professionals

SKN Publishing. ISBN: ISBN 978-0-9569175-0-8.
www.everyday-heroes.co.uk

Published by SKN Publishing

A division of Interims for Development Ltd.

Kingsbury House, 468 Church Lane, London NW9 8UA

A CIP catalogue record for this book is available from the British Library

ISBN: 978-0-9569175-1-5

Cover Image © Prillfoto|Dreamstime.com

Prepared and printed by:

York Publishing Services Ltd
64 Hallfield Road, Layerthorpe, York, YO31 7ZQ
www.yps-publishing.co.uk

For my girls, Seena and Khaya,

who make every day an adventure.

Marina

Best wishes,

[signature]

March '14.

Acknowledgements

In writing this book, I am indebted to many people who have shared their experiences of working in Africa and their expertise in recruiting for Africa.

My sincere thanks go to Carol Hondonga of Rio Tinto for her generosity and time and for her constant willingness to share her passion for Africa with its diaspora. I am grateful to Audrey Mensah of AMSCO for her insights into what recruiters seek – and for co-opting her colleagues into providing their input.

I would also like to thank a number of people who were kind enough to share their stories about the benefits and challenges of working in Africa. They include Elvina Quaison, Simi Belo, Selorm Adadevoh, Bernie Akporiaye and Ernestina Boadi. My thanks also go to the many African executives and HR managers that participated in interviews for ReConnect Africa, and particularly to Keli Gadzekpo, co-founder and CEO of the Databank Group, for his advice and tips for succeeding in Africa.

I am enormously grateful to John Battersby, a staunch African patriot, for his tireless efforts to showcase the best of Africa and to safeguard the brand of South Africa. His kindness in agreeing to write the foreword for this book is indicative of the unfailing support he has shown me over many years.

Last, but most certainly not least, my love and thanks to my family, both near and far, for their constant encouragement and support.

> *"The time for Africa is now."*
>
> Mark Otty, Ernst & Young's
> 2nd Africa Attractiveness survey

Contents

Foreword by John Battersby, UK Country Manager, Brand South Africa

I cannot think of a more timely or practical book for African professionals planning to repatriate their skills and experience or for non-Africans planning to work or invest in the continent which is now poised on the brink of a major economic turnaround.

At a recent seminar of recruiters and Human Resource managers, the extent to which attitudes towards Africa have changed was captured in two spontaneous comments.

The first, a British-born professional of West African descent, confidently and unselfconsciously announced that for the first time in her life "it's cool to be African in London".

The second intervention came right at the end of the seminar from a British professional who after being riveted by the dialogue, announced in her closing remarks: "I am beginning to wish I was African."

Perhaps the greatest indicator of the nature and extent of these changes is the title of this book. No-one in their right mind would have proposed it even a decade ago.

In the ten years I have been based in London, I have seen the fortunes of Africa transformed from what the *Economist* magazine described on its cover as "The hopeless continent" a decade ago to what is now largely acknowledged by investors as the last frontier of growth for the global economy and the world's third-largest market-in-the-making after China and India.

Thirty-five years ago, every major global investor knew that they had to have a foot in the door of China as an investment destination. They didn't always know how to do it or exactly what the risks were, but they knew they had to be there if they were to remain a global player in the future.

One could say the same about Africa today. But the realisation has been slow in coming despite a flood of Africa seminars and conferences held in London since the Commission for Africa back in 2005, focussing new interest on the continent in the UK and changing perceptions about trade and investment opportunities.

Africa has itself reinforced the paradigm with a significant reduction in conflicts, a growing shift towards more transparent economies and a gradual but inexorable gear-change towards more accountable governance. The rapid increase in investment in the continent by China and South Africa and high-growth markets such as India, Turkey, Russia and Brazil, have hastened the process of Africa's rising.

The viral spread of the mobile phone in Africa and the proliferation of internet banking are just two recent indicators of the continent's future growth. Its natural resources, food basket promise and potential for the development of renewable energy all point in the same direction.

But the real potential of Africa lies in its people. The quality of African professionals in the diaspora is proof of that. Not belonging to either the "developed" north or the "developing or high-growth" south, these skilled Africans are uniquely agile in being able to negotiate and leapfrog solutions which have taken decades to develop. It could be seen as the hidden African dividend.

And in an increasingly digitalised and globalised world, there is no reason for those skills, knowledge and experience not to be shared with their home countries on the continent, whether by repatriation or virtual transference.

Organisations like the Homecoming Revolution in South Africa, now targeting five key African countries in south, east, west and central sub-Saharan Africa, AFFORD in the UK with its proactive Africa Gives project, ReConnect Africa, and the UK Africa project are reshaping the role of the African diaspora abroad and redefining the relationship between the diaspora and the continent.

Africans returning to the continent have a unique advantage in terms of knowing how the rest of the world works and how Africa fits into it and can thus develop their own competitive edge in the global economy.

It is this generation of global Africans who are transforming the continent and who will know how to pitch its investment offerings and messages to the industrialised world.

With two decades of experience as a professional coach, skills developer and advocate for African excellence, Frances Mensah Williams has produced an immensely affirmative and practical guide to getting employment in Africa.

John Battersby is the UK Country Manager of Brand South Africa, co-author with David Elliot Cohen of *Mandela: A Life in Photographs* (Sterling 2010) and author of the Afterword in the updated biography of *Nelson Mandela* by Anthony Sampson (Harper Collins 2011).

About the Author

Frances Mensah Williams is a writer, coach and Human Resources consultant with over twenty years experience of developing and managing people, both in the UK and in Africa.

She is the Chief Executive of Interims for Development Ltd., an award-winning UK-based Human Resources, Careers and Training consultancy that has successfully assisted businesses and organisations in Europe and across Africa with HR advisory services, recruitment, executive coaching and talent development programmes.

She is also the publisher and Editor of ReConnect Africa (www.reconnectafrica.com), an online magazine and website providing essential information on careers and business for African professionals in the diaspora.

Frances has worked with leading companies across diverse sectors both in Europe and in Africa. She consults on issues relating to Human Resources management and talent acquisition and development and is an experienced trainer and facilitator. As an Executive Coach, she works with senior level clients globally on career and enterprise development strategies and she speaks and writes extensively on issues relating to skills development in Africa and harnessing the talents of the African Diaspora.

She is the author of the book *'Everyday Heroes – Learning from the Careers of Successful Black Professionals'* and the recipient of numerous awards including the 2010 WE Universal Award for Connecting Africans around the World, the 2009 AYF Adler Award for Media for ReConnect Africa, the 2005 Gold Award for Innovative Capacity Building, the 2005 Black Enterprise Award for Rising Star of the Year and the 2005 GPA Award for Business Innovator of the Year.

In 2011, to mark the 100th anniversary of International Women's Day, Frances Mensah Williams was nominated as one of the *Top 20 Inspirational Females from the Africa Diaspora in Europe* in a list compiled by ADIPWE (African Diaspora Professional Women in Europe).

Introduction

If the number of conferences, forums, summits and events is anything to go by, Africa is, without doubt, the hottest topic on the lips of investors, businesses, non-governmental organisations and entrepreneurs.

In recent years there has been a remarkable turnaround in the Africa story; from a relentlessly negative portrayal of the continent to one that highlights the increasing number of success stories that can be found.

What does this mean for people with an interest in working within this most exciting and diverse of continents? Where Africa was once solely portrayed as a high risk proposition, today's stories of enterprise, creativity, and commercial success have generated a greater desire on the part of both Africans and non-Africans to be part of the economic turnaround of the continent.

At the same time as the global economic crisis and resultant slowdown has hit hard on the jobs market in Europe and the United States, Africa seems to be on the rise. Small wonder, then, that the level of interest in careers in Africa is now so high.

While it is true to say that many African countries offer a wealth of opportunities for a wide range of careers across many sectors, if your career plan includes the opportunity to work within the African continent, you need to plan your approach carefully to give yourself the best chance to identify and get the job you want.

Making a career move to Africa may be the best decision you ever make or it could be a poor choice that sets you back and leaves you feeling bitter and frustrated.

With this book, my intention is to share tips from my own experience as a career coach and a former HR Director in Africa, as well as the advice of many people that I have interviewed over the years, including employers, recruiters and those who have made the career move into Africa.

By keeping in mind the opportunities that the African continent offers and preparing for the challenges it presents, my hope is that our collective wisdom will guide you towards developing the right strategy and taking the best approach to move your career into the world's most exciting continent, Africa.

"If you want to succeed, you should strike out on new paths, rather than travel the worn paths of accepted success."

John D. Rockefeller

Chapter 1

Why Africa?

If you've voiced a desire to work in Africa, you may have been met with curiosity, scepticism, or even disbelief. People are bound to have asked you why you would want to do so, and it's a good question. Indeed, *why* should you consider a career in Africa?

The answer is that, despite its challenges, Africa is a huge and diverse continent that offers exciting and rewarding opportunities for professionals today. But how do you go about breaking into these opportunities? In the following chapters, I will outline some of my suggestions about how you can plan your approach and create a winning strategy to enter the African job market.

To understand the job market in such a diverse continent, it's worth first taking a look at the context in which this market operates.

In May 2000, *The Economist* magazine published an issue with a front page that declared Africa to be 'The Hopeless Continent'. In December 2011, the publication featured another front page devoted to Africa. This time, the caption read: 'Africa Rising'.

These two front pages symbolise the change in the Africa story that has been taking place over the past decade and the truly remarkable shift in the perception and brand of Africa in the business and investment communities. Far from being 'the hopeless continent', Africa is now what the billionaire hedge fund manager George Soros calls "one of the few bright spots on the gloomy global economic horizon".

> *"By the 2040s, we have no doubt that the likes of Nigeria, Ghana, Angola, Egypt, Kenya, Ethiopia and South Africa will be considered among the growth powerhouses of the global economy."*
>
> **Ajen Sita, Ernst & Young's Managing Partner for Africa**

What makes Africa an attractive proposition today? Here's what some organisations have said.

- **Ernst & Young's 3rd Africa Attractiveness Survey** 2013 of more than 500 investors and business leaders noted that, despite the impact of the ongoing global economic situation, the size of the African economy has more than tripled since 2000; the continent's growth outlook appears positive, with African gross domestic product (GDP) as a whole expected to grow by 4% in 2013 and 4.6% in 2014. In 2013, Africa ranked ahead of five other regions for investment attractiveness, beating the former Soviet states, Eastern Europe, Western Europe, the Middle East and Central America. Business leaders with an established presence on the continent ranked Africa as the second most attractive regional investment destination in the world after Asia, with 86% of them saying they believed Africa's attractiveness as a place to do business would continue to improve.

- **The International Monetary Fund** has stated that Africa will have the world's fastest-growing economy of any continent over the next five years. Its forecasts also show that seven of the world's 10 fastest-growing economies will be African, with Ethiopia, Mozambique, Tanzania, Congo, Ghana, Zambia and Nigeria expected to expand by more than 6% a year until 2015.

- **McKinsey's** survey of 15,000 consumers in 10 different African countries found Africans to have the kind of spending habits that attract big companies. According to the report, most African households spent 30% of their money on groceries, 10% on clothing, and 6% on telecommunications.

- **The World Bank** has reported that sub-Saharan Africa grew by 4.9% in 2011 and that for most of the past decade, Africa south of the Sahara has grown faster than Asia.

- **The African Development Bank** has noted early signs of a growth in the continent's middle class and projects that, by 2030, much of the continent will have a middle-class majority and that consumer spending will soar from $680 billion in 2008 to $2.2 trillion.

The level of interest in the continent from the global investment community highlights why Africa is the most exciting space today.

The UNCTAD World Investment Report 2013 gives an interesting overview of foreign direct investment (FDI) into Africa and how the continent is bucking global trends. The report found that while investment in extractive industries remained the most important driver of FDI to Africa in 2012, there was increased investment in consumer-oriented manufacturing and services. This reflects the growing purchasing power of Africa's fast emerging middle class.

The continent is proving attractive not only to traditional investors, but also to companies from emerging markets, and the report showed that the biggest investors in 2012 were, in order of size, Malaysia, South Africa and China. South African companies were increasingly active in acquiring operations in industries such as mining and healthcare during 2012, pushing FDI outflows from South Africa up to $4.4 billion and lifting the country to the position of the largest source country of FDI in Africa.

Energy resources such as recently discovered gas reserves in Tanzania and oil fields in Uganda have seen significant investment flows into East Africa, while investment inflows into Central Africa have been at a record high. The region's natural resources continue to attract investment from mining companies, with significant FDI into the Democratic Republic of the Congo.

The report also found that North Africa was beginning to see a revival in cross-border investment following the political turmoil of 2011, with significant increases in FDI flows into the region.

The Skills Challenge

How does all this translate into opportunities for you in your career journey?

An increase in prosperity brings with it enhanced opportunities for employment, says Donald Gips, a former US Ambassador to South Africa. "This rising prosperity in Africa will create jobs. More and more people understand that the 21st century will be the African century."

Increased prosperity also brings with it the need for skills and expertise and it is impossible to understand the African job market without appreciating the impact of what has been termed Africa's 'brain drain'.

Statistics relating to the African brain drain over the past two decades have not been encouraging. It's been estimated that, since 2000, Africa has lost over 20,000 professionals annually to other parts of the world. Although the causes vary, much of the skills flight has been due to economic migration by Africans seeking higher education and better employment opportunities and by people escaping civil unrest and conflict.

While hard data are difficult to come by, this exodus of skills has included engineers, lawyers, educators, utility workers, health workers, transport operators, retailers, artisans and public servants – essentially, the people with the skills every society needs to safeguard its lives and health and to enable it to function.

Countries including Gambia, Sierra Leone, Mauritius and Cape Verde have seen high migration rates among their university graduate populations. Significant numbers of medical and teaching professionals have left countries such as Ghana and South Africa, while the United States is home to more African scientists than can be found across the entire continent of Africa. Research from the International Organization for Migration, for instance, shows that 33% of physicians born in Lesotho are registered as working abroad.

"The greatest problem facing African businesses today is the immense difficulty of attracting sufficient talent," says Elijah Litheko, Chief Executive Officer of the South African Human Resources professional body, IPM South Africa.

"There are not enough skilled workers to fill the specific needs of the expanding economies of the continent."

When it comes to education, Africa lags behind other regions and, despite the demand for skills in Africa, he says, "Tertiary institutions do not produce enough graduates in business-related fields."

While, more recently, the tide has started to turn with increasing numbers of skilled Africans returning to their home countries to work and set up businesses, there is still a huge deficit in the level of skills needed within these emerging African economies.

Companies operating in Africa readily admit that African professionals abroad who are keen to return home are a critical source of talent for their businesses. Indeed, hiring from this group makes business sense as, according to World Bank estimates, replacing the skills lost from Africa costs more than $4 billion a year in salaries for expatriate human resources.

For employers in Africa, African diaspora professionals bring not only experience of working internationally, but also a knowledge of the culture, markets and languages of their home continent, as well as valuable contacts, connections and networks.

Spotting Career Opportunities

So where, you may wonder, can the career opportunities arising from this boom in Africa's fortunes be found? The short answer is: simply everywhere. Here are some reasons why:

- The African continent contains the world's biggest deposits of platinum, diamonds and manganese. It's also a significant producer of oil, coal, copper and bauxite, which is used to make aluminium. Also, alongside the traditional exports of oil, natural gas and minerals, the output from manufactured goods has doubled over the past decade.

- The impact of technology has revolutionised the way business can now be done. According to the GSMA, the association that represents the interests of mobile operators worldwide, Africa is now the world's second largest mobile market by connections after Asia, and the fastest growing mobile market in the world. The next few years will be pivotal for the telecommunications sector in Africa as new investments flow in and infrastructure is further developed.

- The mobile phone has led not only to increased connectivity across the continent, but to innovative approaches to banking, accessing cash and making payments and creating new opportunities in financial services. Of the world's top 20 countries using mobile banking, 15 are African. In Kenya, for example, only two years after the mobile banking system M-PESA was introduced by Safaricom in 2007, 40% of Kenya's adult population had joined its customer base, making the M-PESA service the most popular in Kenya.

Mobile money has become a popular platform across Africa as a whole, offering enhanced convenience and security, as well bringing previously unbanked sections of society into the financial system.

- Ernst & Young's 3rd Africa Attractiveness Survey found that, despite perceptions to the contrary, less than one-third of Africa's growth is coming from natural resources. While mining and metals continue to offer growth potential, the trend today is one of growing diversification with an increasing emphasis on services, manufacturing and infrastructure-related activities. Other sectors where there has been a noticeable shift in interest include ICT, financial services and education. According to the survey, services accounted for 70% of Africa's FDI projects in 2012 (up from 45% in 2007), while manufacturing activities accounted for 43% of capital invested in 2012 (up from 22% in 2007).

"The greatest problem facing African businesses today is the immense difficulty of attracting sufficient talent."

**Elijah Litheko, CEO, IPM South Africa,
'Africa's Talent Challenge'
(WorldLink May 2013 – WFPMA)**

Looking to Africa for opportunities is a worthwhile bet, says Peter Guest, the award-winning journalist and editor and the author of the book, '*Africa's Century*'.

"The fact that so much of the continent is blossoming at a time when the rest of the world is going through its own economic hardship is showing people that the benefits of taking a risk on unstructured – but growing – markets is worthwhile. I do think that people associate Africa with growth and opportunity more than ever before. This will be the century when African countries, and Africa as an entity, moves to take its place in a world that has been governed by historical inequities for a long time."

When asked which countries he sees as offering stand-out opportunities, Guest says: "So much of the opportunity depends on your sector and appetite for risk. For sheer size, no one should ignore Nigeria. But then you have Ghana, which is a phenomenal prospect for the right company.

"Cote d'Ivoire is a real recovery play too. In the east, the whole EAC could be a major destination. If you are more adventurous, somewhere like South Sudan, the world's newest country, is a real growth play. There is not a great deal there, to be blunt, and people have the same aspirations as anywhere else."

A number of factors point toward tremendous economic growth going forward. Driven by the demands of a rapidly emerging middle class, consumer spending is currently estimated to be more than 60% of sub-Saharan Africa's GDP.

There is also a luxury market developing in the continent. In Kenya, for example, the number of households where the head holds higher managerial, professional or administrative positions is expected to grow by 28% between 2011 and 2020, according to data from Euromonitor International. Over the same period, China is expected to grow 4%, while Russia is expected to contract 2%.

The rapid changes in Africa and other nations in the global South have led to what many see as a shift in economic power away from developed economies. This transformation has led, in turn, to a shift in perception of where opportunities lie.

John Battersby, UK Country Manager for Brand South Africa, points out that "Many African economies are growing faster than those in Europe and some European countries – such as Spain, Greece and Portugal – now have higher levels of unemployment than some African countries, and many of the world's leading companies have emerged from the so-called developing world."

"Africa,", he says, "with its rich mineral and natural resources, growing trend towards accountable government, economic transparency and co-ordinated development is increasingly being seen as the last frontier of the global economy. The continent has long been regarded by high-growth economies such as China, India, Brazil and Turkey as a key economic partner. Africa still has a long way to go in terms of developing strong regional markets and becoming an integrated continental market, but when it achieves more acceptable levels of integration, it will be the world's third largest functioning market after China and India."

While there are still areas of political and economic instability in some parts of the African continent, the old narrative of a hopeless Africa plagued with problems has changed to one of rising economic prosperity.

The Good News for Careers

So what does all this mean for you as you consider moving your career to Africa?

Successful careers can best be developed within successful organisations and, unlike North America, Europe and much of East Asia, the African continent offers promising signs of the long-term growth that companies need to prosper. Africa is now nearly as urbanised as China and there are as many cities with a population exceeding one million in Africa as there are in Europe.

A report from the McKinsey Global Institute, '*Africa at Work: Job Creation and Inclusive Growth*', predicts that, if economies continue to grow, Africa could create up to 72 million wage-paying jobs by 2020, with more than half of these from agriculture, manufacturing, retail and hospitality – sectors in which graduates are relatively scarce. Over the past decade Africa has created over 37 million wage-paying jobs and a key challenge for the continent is to accelerate the pace of jobs needed to meet its expanding labour pool and consumer class.

There is a need for skilled employees for these jobs but there is still a huge disparity between the quality of education currently offered to students in sub-Saharan Africa and the needs of its industries and the local job markets.

Despite its huge deposits of natural resources, for example, Africa has the lowest percentage of engineering graduates in the world, and new graduates from African universities are often perceived as costly and lacking in relevant experience and job readiness skills. This has led many companies to turn to professionals, and especially those of African origin, who have been studying and working abroad.

Spotting career opportunities in Africa is not difficult, says Keli Gadzekpo, co-founder and CEO of African financial services firm, Databank, a company he was instrumental in setting up in Ghana after a successful career in the United States.

"People need to be fully aware that Africa offers what I would call frontier economies. So, in my view, every single skill set needed in developed economies is needed here. Of course, there is a case of prioritising which is the most immediately needed. We are still at a level where core skills can make a difference; for example, good solid banking and insurance skills. You need to evaluate productive sectors; in Ghana the services sector i.e. tourism, ICT, etc. all offer opportunities, and we have a comparative advantage in agriculture. New media, marketing, and so on, are also areas where, in my view, Africa should push forward."

While the brain drain from Africa has been a major impediment to the rate of the continent's development, like every catastrophe, there is a silver lining. When it comes to career opportunities, there are a number of ways in which the brain drain and Africa's prospects for growth have combined to provide you with greater opportunities for better jobs than ever before.

In short:

- Many African countries are reforming their economies; national leaders are developing economic policies that seek to avoid past mistakes, and the prospects for growth continue to look positive.

- Many countries have under-skilled populations, making it difficult for companies to expand their operations and scale.

- There is a dearth of management and specialist skills available to businesses and governments across the continent

- Increased investment from China and elsewhere is helping to improve infrastructure and creating new business opportunities across both traditional and new sectors

- The impact of mobile technology had created a raft of new opportunities for business growth which, in turn, needs skills

Africa today has 54 countries, some with greater challenges than others, yet all offering some opportunity for taking your career forward.

But before you rush to book your flight, take a deep breath and ask yourself: are you ready?

> *"No, no! The adventures first; explanations take such a dreadful time."*

Lewis Carroll, Alice's Adventures in Wonderland & Through the Looking-Glass

Chapter 2

What's my Motivation?

I've outlined some of the many reasons why you should consider a career in Africa and why the continent offers such exciting prospects. But, like any adventure, you need to be clear why you are going and give some thought to what you expect to find.

Before you rush into the adventure that is Africa, it is critical that you stop and consider your own reasons for doing so.

Identifying What's Driving Me

If you decided to move house, you would probably have good reasons to justify the expense and upheaval involved. It might be that you need a bigger house to accommodate a growing family, or that your current home is too far from work and costing you too much in time and travel. You might perhaps be surrounded by noisy neighbours who are affecting the quality of your life, or feel that you are living too far from other family members.

As you make the decision to move country – a far bigger undertaking than moving house – it's important that you are clear about the reasons why. Interviews that I recently conducted with people who have relocated to Africa identified a range of different motives for making the move.

Some of the reasons cited included:

- *'I wanted a greater chance to progress my career'*

- *'I wanted to be back home and to live closer to my extended family in Africa'*

- *'I was fed up of living and working in the West'*

- *'I wanted to work in a different culture to boost my professional experience'*

- *'I believed there were better professional opportunities than in the UK'*

- *'An overseas assignment is important to progress within my company'*

- *'I consider Africa as my spiritual and cultural home'*

- *'I wanted to return to the continent I was born in and make a difference with the skills I gained abroad'*

One or more of these reasons may also apply to you. Why is it so important that you analyse your motivation? Quite simply, the clearer you are about your motivation, the better able you will be to position yourself to attract the right employers, as well as to make the mental adjustments necessary to deal with such a huge change to your life. In short, if you are clear about why you are in Africa, you will be able to deal far better with the challenges as and when they arise.

It's likely that you know of people who have gone to work in Africa. Some may be positive about their decision and excited about the possibilities now open to them; others may share horror stories of sluggish African bureaucracies, a poor work ethic, a pervasive lack of urgency, and an unwillingness to help those coming into the country.

> *"My motivation was a combination of emotional and practical. I had a strong sense of home when I visited Ghana and, on the practical side, I could see there was a great deal of opportunity in the flourishing new developing Ghana than was available in the UK."*
>
> **Elvina Quaison, MD, Silk Solutions, Ghana**

The challenge you face to become one of the success stories and to navigate the tougher aspects of working in Africa's developing economies will be more easily overcome when you are clear as to why it matters to you.

Separating Romance from Realism

Much as you may want to race off on your adventure to Africa, be practical and check if you have packed enough of the right things to take with you.

The first of these, I would suggest, is a healthy dose of realism. Having analysed why you want to go to Africa, it's also important to address why you don't want to stay where you are.

Is it because you can't find a job? Are you frustrated from hitting a glass ceiling that you can't seem to rise above in your current job? Are you under-employed, given your academic achievements? Do you feel your ethnicity is a block to your ambitions at work? Are you tired of working in jobs that don't add up to a career path? Are your friends or former schoolmates in Africa doing much better than you and making you feel inadequate?

> *"Have a very clear idea of why you are moving to Africa. Otherwise, it will be easy to pack and run back when the going gets tough."*
>
> **Bernie Akporiaye, Senegal**

In other words, are you drawn towards something positive or running away from something? If it's the latter; again, be clear. If you don't address the real issues underlying your desire to move, you could simply be transporting your problems with you.

Unless you are very lucky, moving your career to Africa will not be straightforward or easy. You will have to handle a host of issues, both emotional and practical, so it's important that you take off your rose-tinted glasses and put aside the romantic vision of Africa that you may be harbouring so you can deal with the reality that you will face.

Let's look at some of the possible ideas you may have about working in Africa and how realistic these are.

Myths and Misconceptions

Something else to put into your travel bag for your adventure is the antidote to all those things that you think you know about a place. By this, I mean all your assumptions. Sometimes, and particularly when we are swayed by the romance of a new adventure, it's hard to look past the picture that we have built up in our minds.

There are many myths and misconceptions about living and working in Africa, not least because the continent is so diverse that people's experiences can be very different, even within the same country.

Bernie Akporiaye, an experienced IT professional of Nigerian origin who lived and worked in the UK for many years before deciding to move to Senegal, points out that people outside Africa can have grave misconceptions about the continent.

"People often assume that there is an uneducated and unsophisticated market here," he says. "Some people think that it's easy to make your mark and achieve success because you are bringing all these skills. Another popular misconception is that everyone is poor, corrupt or starving."

The assumption that an extravagant lifestyle is immediately available to an experienced professional who moves to Africa is another myth that people should reject, says Elvina Quaison, following her move to Ghana to set up a business after a successful career in London.

"Sometimes people assume that they will fall into a lovely expat package and that they will be considered special just by virtue of being foreign," she says. "There's also this underlying assumption that everyone in Africa is lazy and inept."

This myth is one that is echoed by Keli Gadzekpo, CEO of the Databank Group, a leading financial services firm headquartered in Ghana.

"I would say that the main misconceptions people outside Africa have is that they are technically superior to the locals, that our systems here should function as they do abroad, and that locals don't know what they are doing."

> *"A big myth is that business in Africa is so backward that there is a blank slate to write on and that expats are required to build everything from scratch. Not true! So much exists and is established already in Africa."*
>
> **Simi Belo, Nigeria**

However, some misconceptions can lead to pleasant surprises, says Ernestina Boadi, an Events Management professional now working in Ghana.

"I was concerned about a lack of social life once I moved, but the diversity and variety of social circles here has really surprised me. There is such an international population here," she says of life in Accra. "I also thought the economy would be difficult, but I've been pleasantly surprised to see that the economy is buoyant and growing."

Not having spent much time on research before making her move to Africa, what has surprised her has been the high cost of living. "I didn't expect it to be so costly to live and, for example, I find that a substantial percentage of my income is spent on transport," she admits.

Recruiters at African management services organisation, AMSCO, interview many people who are looking for work in Africa. A key misconception that they encounter is the idea that "the flow of things is the same as in the developed world, and that things happen as and when they want them to." The reality, they point out, is that in Africa it is difficult to control timing and things will move much more slowly than people might be used to.

Nevertheless, moving your career to Africa does not signal the end of your professional journey, says Carol Hondonga, a senior advisor on talent management for Africa for the global mining and metals giant Rio Tinto. "A big misconception is that going to Africa is a final destination and a dead end." In fact, the skills and experience that you gain can make you highly marketable across a number of sectors and greatly improve your prospects if you eventually decide to move elsewhere.

How do you envisage your life will be when you move to Africa? And how can you get to the truth behind some of the myths or misconceptions that you may have built up? Doing your research into the country that you are considering moving to will help give you a more realistic picture of what awaits you, and we'll look at this in more detail in the coming chapters.

Who's My Competition?

As you consider your career adventure into Africa, it's worth bearing in mind that you are planning to enter a very competitive jobs market – yet another reason to be sure that you are really motivated to make the move.

If you originate from Africa, bear in mind that while there can be a strong strategic interest on the part of companies in Africa to recruit professionals of African origin, the fact is that employers and businesses are predominantly interested in skills, no matter who has them.

The demand for skills, particularly in key, specialised sectors, has led to a substantial influx of different nationalities into the corporate landscape in Africa. Thus, while Africans abroad are increasingly looking for career opportunities in Africa, they are not the only ones motivated to work there.

Where particular skills may be relatively scarce, companies in Africa that are not able to meet their recruitment needs from within their local market will search for the best and brightest from the global marketplace. Moreover, as more companies expand into the fast emerging markets within Africa, creating a greater need for skilled staff, there will be even more interest from non-Africans who see working in Africa as a development opportunity for their careers.

Indeed, studies conducted among students and young professionals in the United States and in Europe have shown that international work experience is high on the list for many of them, and that a large percentage expects to live and work abroad at some point in their career. Many young professionals see the advantages of cross-cultural experience for their professional development, particularly when it comes to working in international organisations, and are open to working in a new country for a job opportunity, even when they have never visited that country. Industries such as oil and gas, engineering and pharmaceuticals, for example, often have international career routes that involve working overseas.

Research has shown that the so-called Generation Y or Millennials (those born between the early 1980s and the early 2000's) are increasingly more likely to see themselves as global citizens and are interested in working and experiencing new markets and cultures. Where previous generations of Western professionals would usually take on overseas assignments in more senior roles during the later stages of their careers, the millennial generation is more likely to look for opportunities to work abroad within the early years of their careers.

In recent years, citizens of many different countries, all united in their desire to identify career and business opportunities in emerging economies, have been moving into Africa. Record levels of investment in Africa from China have also brought many Chinese nationals to the continent in search of opportunities. While these include unskilled and semi-skilled labour, the growth and expansion of Chinese companies and Chinese-funded infrastructure has also seen the arrival of skilled migrants seeking wider opportunities.

Carol Hondonga, a senior executive with Rio Tinto, points out that "With the penetration of the Chinese on the continent, Mandarin language capability will become a necessity for effective business partnerships."

Indian businesses such as TATA and Airtel have also been investing heavily in African countries, and the number of skilled Indian professionals seeking jobs outside their own competitive job markets at home, are on the rise.

"Indians are going to African countries like Kenya, Tanzania, South Africa, Ghana, Nigeria, Sudan and Zambia," says Aparajita Biswas, a professor at the Centre for African Studies, University of Mumbai, who introduced a self-financing, six-month course on international trade between India and Africa to help equip Indians going to African countries for work. The attendees on her course – young people, businessmen and government employees –

illustrate the increasing interest in Africa from people of different backgrounds. Countries such as Ghana are viewed favourably because of their economic and political stability and the safe working environment that they offer.

East and Southern Africa are proving an increasingly popular choice for Indian and Chinese professionals seeking positions in finance, retail, sales and marketing. Expatriate salaries and benefits are a popular draw and, as localisation policies in other regions make it harder for foreign nationals to secure well-paid roles, Africa has become an increasingly attractive option.

> *"I thought the economy would be difficult, but I've been pleasantly surprised to see that the economy is buoyant and growing."*
>
> **Ernestina Boadi**

Another source of competition for jobs in Africa are African professionals who have made their way back to their home countries, or to other African countries, armed with qualifications and experience gained from working abroad across a wide range of sectors.

Although figures vary, there is an undeniable increase in the number of expatriate Africans returning to their countries in what some observers see as the slow reversal of the brain drain from the continent.

A number of factors are contributing to this influx, including the ongoing impact of the global economic crisis and the resulting downturn in jobs in Europe and the United States. Some other factors behind this trend are the desire to be back in their home culture and closer to extended family, the perception of enjoying a better and more balanced lifestyle in Africa than in the West, and the desire to use the skills and experience acquired abroad to both help Africa's development and secure better careers.

In a survey conducted for our online careers publication, ReConnect Africa.com, 98.5% of the African professionals who responded said they were actively considering returning to work in Africa. These findings are echoed by the results of a survey run by private equity firm Jacana across 10 US and European business schools. Responses to that survey showed that 3 out of 4 of the African students hoped to work in Africa after graduating.

Competition for career opportunities also comes from within Africa as more African professionals choose to move their careers into other African countries, a process facilitated by the free movement of labour afforded by regional blocs such as ECOWAS and SADC. Freedom to work across the job markets within these blocs has led to the movement of high-skilled labour into countries seen as stable and prosperous.

In short, world class skills are already in Africa or are making their way there. How will you measure up? In a competitive job market, you will need to be proactive and savvy in your approach to get the job you want.

As we move on to look at your job search strategy, and bearing in mind global interest in the continent, how can you best position yourself for the African job market?

"When I'm hiring someone I look for magic and a spark. Little things that intuitively give me a gut feeling that this person will go to the ends of the earth to accomplish the task at hand."

Tommy Mottola

Chapter 3

Who's Hiring?

If, after thinking through your motivation and understanding your competition, you're still convinced that you want to work in Africa, the next question to consider is: who exactly is going to hire you?

While a number of multinational companies based in the USA and Europe have a long history of providing employment in Africa, home grown African corporations have increasingly extended their reach across the continent and into new markets. Companies like SABMiller, Richemont, Dangote, MTN Group, Naspers, Standard Bank Group, Old Mutual, Discovery Holdings, Ecobank, Liberty Life Group, Nando's and the Shoprite Group are all well established across the African continent.

Employers in Africa come from a wide variety of industries and sectors, some of which are highlighted in this chapter.

Oil and Gas

Oil and Gas is Africa's major industry and a sector which has boomed in the last decade and seen remarkable advances in offshore technology. Africa's oil and gas production has grown steadily, with Nigeria, Angola and other key producers accounting for almost 10% of global oil production. Today, Nigeria is the world's 13th largest oil producer.

The strength of this sector looks set to continue as new discoveries continue to be made in the Gulf of Guinea and off the coast of Mozambique and Tanzania, while new investment in infrastructure will see this sector's contribution to growth continue across a number of countries. Although the majority of oil and gas reserves and production are concentrated in countries such as Nigeria, Libya, Algeria, Angola, Sudan and Egypt, production from countries such as Ghana and Uganda has added to the rapid growth to be found in this sector.

The African oil and gas boom has been fuelled by demand from China, and two-thirds of China's imports from Africa – predominantly from Angola, now the second largest oil producer in sub-Saharan Africa, and Sudan – are crude oil. More than nineteen African countries are significant producers of oil and/or gas – in Mozambique alone, gas reserves estimated at over 60 trillion cubic metres have already been found – and this sector offers career opportunities in countries as diverse as Kenya, Mali, Sierra Leone and Somalia.

> *"Many of South Africa's major employers are in the mining sector, with more than one million people in mining-related employment. Two of the world's largest mining companies have their origins in South Africa."*

Where this sector was once dominated by major corporations such as Shell, Exxon Mobil and Total, the discovery, exploration and production of oil and gas in Africa have seen the rise of new operators such as Tullow Oil, Cobalt International, Anadarko and Ophir Energy. Over the next two decades, activity in this sector looks set to grow and oil and gas will continue to offer career opportunities in Africa for some time to come.

Mining

Mining has played a crucial role in the economic development of Africa for a long time and the major players that have dominated this sector include multinational companies such as Rio Tinto, Anglo American, Barrick and BHP Billiton.

Mining companies are well established in many African countries, with some, such as in the DRC, partially owned by their governments. Mining projects are often long-term and highly capitalised, and one such project, the BHP Billiton Xstrata joint venture in South Africa, the Douglas-Middleburg Optimisation Coal project, is worth ZAR 9.3 billion and is expected to provide profits for the mining companies in Africa until 2034.

Mining plays a crucial role in Africa's socio-economic development. In South Africa, for example, it accounts for a third of the Johannesburg Stock Market's market capitalisation. Across the continent, almost 2000 mining projects are at various phases from grassroots through to operational. Zimbabwe and South Africa actively mine coal, with roughly 4.9% of the global coal reserve concentrated in South Africa. Coal, copper, diamonds and uranium are heavily mined within the continent and today South Africa is the world's largest producer of a wide range of gems and minerals.

Many of South Africa's major employers are in this sector, with more than one million people in mining-related employment. Two of the world's largest mining companies have their origins in South Africa; BHP Billiton, which was the result of a merger between South Africa's Billiton and the Australian BHP Group, and Anglo American Plc., which has a primary listing on the London Stock Exchange and a secondary listing in Johannesburg.

In Ghana, mining accounts for 5% of the country's GDP and is largely focused on gold, along with diamonds, bauxite and manganese. There are over 20 companies actively mining in Ghana, with AngloGold Ashanti as the key player within the industry.

In Zambia, mining has mostly centred on the extraction of copper, gold and gems, with large uranium mining projects underway. Botswana – where diamond mining produces 70% of the country's export earnings – and Angola are Africa's largest diamond producers, while Tanzania's mining industry, initially focused around gold, today has sizeable mineral mining projects underway.

The mining sector has also driven the development of a number of related industries that are either suppliers to the mining industry, or users of its products. These include energy, financial services, water and engineering services, and specialist seismic geological and metallurgical services. With its vast untapped mineral resources, Africa looks set to provide jobs and career opportunities in this sector for quite some time.

Banking and Finance

Africa's banking sector has seen a major increase in products, services and regulation in recent years. In the early 1980's the banking industry in much of Africa was dominated by foreign and state-owned banks, with few commercial banks owned and managed by the African private sector.

Sub-Saharan Africa is now one of the world's fastest growing emerging banking markets, and wireless and other technological advances have enabled the development of African and international banking and non-banking financial institutions across the continent offering a wide range of services.

As the continent's economies have expanded on the back of soaring oil and mineral prices, steadily increasing consumer affluence continues to create demand for banking services. Banks are increasing their activity in the area of mergers and acquisitions as they seek to increase their strategic coverage and tap into this demand.

In terms of investment banking, Africa still accounts for only a small amount of activity. However, the rapidly rising economies, particularly across key sub-Saharan countries, are leading to more capital markets and advisory activity. According to *The Banker* publication, the volume of Africa-targeted mergers and acquisitions reached $20 billion in the first half of 2013, up 30% from the same period a year earlier.

Africa's growth prospects and its increasing integration with global financial markets make it a desirable place for investment bankers. Countries such as Namibia, Nigeria and Rwanda have sold Eurobonds, with other sovereign funds planning to follow suit. In countries such as Nigeria, there has been extensive consolidation within the banking sector, creating more advisory opportunities for investment banks.

South Africa's banks dominate Africa's banking landscape and are the largest lenders in Africa, but others are starting to make considerable headway within the sector. Banks such as Zenith Bank, First Bank of Nigeria, National Bank of Egypt, Ecobank, and United Bank for Africa (UBA) have joined South African institutions like the Standard Bank Group, First Rand, Nedbank and Investec in the top rankings in Africa. Morocco's Attijariwafa is the second biggest non-South African lender on the continent after fellow Moroccan bank Groupe Banque Populaire, while Angola's banks are also undergoing rapid expansion.

Within Africa, Nigeria's banking sector is a strong performer. The consolidation of banks and regulatory reform within the sector led to a significant reduction in the number of banks, from what had been almost 90 banks a decade ago to today where the Nigerian banking sector is dominated by five big lenders – Access Bank, First Bank, Guaranty Trust Bank, UBA and Zenith.

Despite a population of 160 million people in Nigeria, there are only about 30 million bank accounts, and banks see considerable scope for growth as well as opportunities for retail lending and corporate banking. New banking channels such as mobile phones offer new routes to attract business, while many industries important to the economy, such as agriculture, remain underfunded. The Nigerian government's planned privatisation drive is also expected to lead to lending opportunities for banks, particularly in the power sector.

ICT/Telecommunications

It's probably safe to say that no other sector has seen such rapid change and societal impact in recent times in Africa as the ICT/Telecoms sector. Since 2000, the telecommunications sector has seen a range of innovative applications that amount to a revolution in ICT within the continent. Innovations such as mobile money transactions, which involve the use of mobile phones as banking tools for transfer and payment, have grown rapidly and have transformed the money transfer market in Africa and abroad. The importance of this sector to the continent's development has resulted in significant government and private sector efforts to develop ICT in Africa.

In the past decade US$150 billion has been invested into African telecoms infrastructure and this sector is a huge and growing market for many telecoms companies. There are now more than 10 submarine cables reaching sub-Saharan Africa, with significant investment going into the deployment of terrestrial fibre optic networks to connect African countries to each other and to the submarine points. Much of the investment to date, heavily supported by financing from China, has gone into countries such as South Africa, Egypt, Algeria, Nigeria and Kenya, while plans are underway to extend this to other sub-Saharan African countries.

Alongside multinational telecommunications companies with operations across the continent, regulatory changes have opened the door for competitive African operators, with more than forty companies now operating across the continent. Mobile banking and other applications have seen Africa overtake and leapfrog Western countries.

The mobile industry currently contributes more than 6% of Sub-Saharan Africa's gross domestic product and this contribution is expected to rise to more than 8% of GDP by 2020, according to a study by GSMA. In 2012, the mobile ecosystem directly supported 3.3 million jobs in the region and contributed $21 billion to public funding, including licence fees. Their report shows that by 2020, mobile is set to double its economic effect and its impact on job opportunities, employing 6.6 million people in sub-Saharan Africa.

Between 2000 and 2012, mobile subscriptions grew to over 700 million and, according to Informa Telecoms and Media, are expected to grow to 1 billion by 2015. In the mobile telecommunications field, Airtel, MTN and Liquid Telecom are the key players, with Airtel covering 14 countries within Africa. Other significant operators include Tigo and Vodacom.

Along with Nigeria and South Africa, Mozambique now stands among the top three countries in the Sub-Saharan Africa to have a modern telecommunication network infrastructure. In a highly competitive market, Movitel is a leading company in the sector, employing nearly 20,000 local people who work as company agents, sales staff, building contractors and station guards.

According to research conducted by Manifest Mind, a sustainability research and consulting company based in the United States, the African mobile telecom market is forecast to grow from a combined value of over US$60 billion in 2013 to a value in 2020 of almost US$234 billion. While much has been achieved in this sector, there is still more to be done to reduce the digital divide between Africa and other parts of the world. If this is a sector of interest for you, these large multinational operators, and their distributers and retailers, will continue to have a need for skills and talented personnel as they grow.

While Kenya, the home of the market leading product, M-PESA, is the most mature market for mobile based financial services, in terms of growth in African mobile subscriptions by carrier, Nigeria has proved to be the most lucrative market. MTN Nigeria is the largest and the fastest growing mobile operator in Africa and the Central Bank of Nigeria reported that in 2013, licensed mobile payment operators had recorded 1.7 million transactions which were worth over 10 billion naira in total. The second and the third fastest growing mobile operators in Africa – Zain Nigeria and EMTS – are also based in Nigeria.

> *"At the end of 2Q-2013, the total subscriptions in Africa reached 863 million – a strong growth of 9.3% year-on-year, which is substantially more robust than other regions around the world."*
>
> **Research by Manifest Mind, LLC**

Another key sector for employment in Africa is **Agriculture**, which accounts for a significant part of the economies of African countries. According to the World Bank, agriculture employs 65% of Africa's labour force and accounts for 32% of gross domestic product. In Nigeria, for example, agriculture accounts for approximately 40% of the economy. While African farm yields are among the lowest globally, African governments are increasingly prioritising the sector with investment programmes aimed at creating opportunities for African farmers in domestic, regional and international markets.

In its '*Africa Agriculture Status Report*', AGRA (the Alliance for a Green Revolution in Africa) points out that the key factors needed to progress the agricultural sector in countries such as Sierra Leone, Liberia, Mali, Burkina Faso and others, are the skills needed to support the use of technology. "Every major review of agricultural R&D…. has highlighted the urgent need to strengthen Africa's human and institutional capacity for agricultural innovation and the importance of increasing the capacity of African agricultural scientists."

Tourism is a key sector in Africa and, according to the World Bank, accounted directly or indirectly for one in every 20 jobs in Sub Saharan Africa in 2011. The region is outpacing all others in tourism growth and countries including Cape Verde, Kenya, Mauritius, Namibia, Rwanda, South Africa and Tanzania have simplified their tourism policies, liberalised air transport and diversified tourism, successfully creating a positive investment climate for tourism development.

Speaking about his company's acquisition of Protea Hotels, the largest hotel group in sub-Saharan Africa, Marriott International CEO Arne Sorenson remarked that the African continent "has significant untapped potential for travel and tourism, both as a destination and a source of new global travellers."

If the development of this sector continues to be managed efficiently over time, tourism has the potential to accelerate job creation and career opportunities in Africa.

> *"Tourism accounted directly or indirectly for one in every 20 jobs in sub-Saharan Africa in 2011, and is one of the few industries on the continent in which women are well represented as employees and managers."*
>
> ***Tourism in Africa: Harnessing Tourism for Growth and Improved Livelihoods***
> **(The World Bank)**

Professional Services present another key sector for employment, covering a number of activities including Management Consultancy, Accountancy, Legal and Engineering. Professional services play an important role in Africa's economies and are among the fastest growing services sectors within the continent. As Africa's economies grow, the demand for business skills and legal and accounting services will increase even further.

A number of international professional services firms such as Ernst & Young and Deloitte have established offices within the continent and the African consultancy market is rapidly expanding, offering career opportunities for qualified professionals.

Healthcare, Infrastructure, Education, Manufacturing, Retail, Hospitality and **Fast Moving Consumer Goods (FMCG)** are also key sectors for growth and career opportunities.

Economic growth in Africa has led to greater disposable incomes and a corresponding rise in consumer demand. With comparatively little growth in developed markets, Africa has become an attractive market for global FMCG firms seeking to expand their operations.

The Public, Private and Third Sectors

When thinking about potential employers in Africa, it's important to consider all the sectors that could offer you the kind of opportunity you are seeking.

While it often has a lower profile than other sectors, **the public sector** is a major and, in some countries, the biggest employer to be found. Public sector roles can be national, regional or even international and can offer opportunities to build relationships and contacts across a wide range of industries.

African governments today broadly see their role as developing market-friendly economies that allow the growth and development of the private sector. To achieve this, governments aim to provide the necessary social and physical infrastructure, and to implement policies and regulatory frameworks that enable private sector economic activity and good governance, all of which require skilled and competent administration.

Indeed, as governments rely increasingly on the private sector to provide services which they themselves once provided, they need to employ within the public sector the type of skills needed to regulate and manage public-private partnerships, as well as their own newly privatised sectors.

African countries are aware of the need to develop an efficient and well functioning public sector to keep pace with the changing political, social and economic environment. This includes the need for a strong civil service, given its role as one of the key institutions charged with formulating and implementing government policies and programmes.

Although the public sector in Africa is often labelled as bureaucratic and a less than dynamic environment in which to work, a number of African authorities have undertaken major reform programmes to improve government efficiency and to build the capacity and professionalism of their ministries and regulatory bodies.

Public sector job opportunities in African countries can include management roles within the civil service, roles as a public servant in central and local government, as well as a range of public administration and management positions.

Some countries have put in place government agencies that deal with recruiting for the civil service and public sector positions. In the city of Durban, South Africa, for example, the eThekwini Metro Municipality has launched an online recruitment system, e- Careers, which provides a paperless recruitment process for the city, and is web-based, which means that people from all over the world can access it. Job seekers can access the system and register to use it via www.durban.gov.za.

A key challenge for governments in Africa is how to attract the best human resources, particularly at local level, to effectively implement government policies and programmes, and particularly those related to the achievement of the internationally agreed development goals.

If you have the skills and experience needed to move into public sector management and to assist the continent to meet its development challenges, this is definitely a sector that you should explore.

> *"A key challenge for governments in Africa is how to attract the best human resources to serve, particularly at local level, to effectively implement government policies and programmes, and particularly those related to the achievement of the internationally agreed development goals."*

If your preference is to work within **the private sector**, Africa offers an exciting place in which to develop your career.

The private sector, often referred to by African governments as the engine of growth, is seen as the most important source of economic growth and job creation on the continent. While official development assistance (aid flows from governments to poorer countries) to Africa and other parts of the world has fallen, foreign direct investment has risen substantially.

In Africa, the private sector has a critical role to play. In 2012, official development aid to the developing world amounted to $135 billion, while $514 billion – three times this amount – went in the form of foreign direct investment, a reflection of the increasing importance of investment rather than aid to Africa's development.

Despite the rapid economic growth that has been seen in a number of African economies, employment growth has not kept apace and, especially in sub-Saharan Africa, there has been limited job creation in the sectors that contribute the most to national GDP. One obstacle, as we have already observed, is the mismatch of skills between labour supply and demand, with many companies unable to find people with the up-to-date knowledge and experience they need, while many countries simply have inadequate capacity.

Business is the main driver of job creation and private sector employers in Africa range in size from established multinational corporations to small and medium sized African companies. Employers cover a wide range of sectors including retail, finance, manufacturing, transportation, construction, oil and gas, healthcare and education.

Some of the larger companies, such as Unilever, Barclays, Diageo and Standard Chartered Bank, are global corporations that have been operating in Africa for many years, while others, such as Ecobank and MTN, Africa's largest mobile operator, were set up as African corporations and have expanded their footprint into key markets across the continent.

Other sources of job opportunities include management services companies and specialist agencies that recruit experienced professionals for fixed-term contracts for companies in Africa. An example of this is AMSCO (African Management Services Company).

African businesses across the continent are creating tens of thousands of jobs, opening up career opportunities in many of the growing economies.

"There is a great mismatch between the region's development needs and the type of graduates it produces each year. The shortage of skills permeates nearly all skill levels, and could get worse as the region's economy continues to grow over the next two decades."

Ken Opalo

The **third sector** is one of the most competitive sectors for employment as it draws in interested candidates from all over the globe. Some people who want to work in Africa are motivated by the desire to give back in some way and to contribute to the development of the continent, while others see the opportunity for an international dimension to their career path.

The African continent is the biggest recipient of international development aid in the world and over the past three decades, the third sector has grown into a multi-billion dollar industry ranging from large international organisations to small, grassroots enterprises. Whether through official development aid from the governments of developed nations or through donor funded non-governmental organisations (NGOs), the aid and humanitarian industry has grown into a major source of careers and jobs in Africa.

Charities and NGOs cover a diverse range of sectors and causes including humanitarian aid, food security, maternal and child health, water supply and hygiene and sanitation. International development organisations also undertake a range of activities intended to improve and enhance good development practices in Africa, inform policy engagement, and increase the global public's understanding of African development challenges.

The financial crisis and euro zone turmoil has led many governments to implement austerity measures, resulting in a reduction in some aid budgets – development aid fell by 4% in real terms in 2012, following a 2% fall in 2011 – including aid to the African continent. The largest aid donors, by volume, are the United States, the United Kingdom, Germany, France and Japan. Denmark, Luxembourg, the Netherlands, Norway and Sweden exceed the United Nations' ODA target of 0.7% of GNI and are heavily involved in NGO activity.

NGOs see their role as non-political, non-ideological and not-for-profit associations dedicated to making the world a better place for the less fortunate. Their aim is to promote community engagement and to improve access to basic social services for disadvantaged members of society.

NGOs generally focus on advocating for particular issues and some are set up by donors to respond to specific causes or to oversee the disbursement of funds or state services.

Careers in international development can also be pursued within multilateral institutions like the World Bank and its private sector arm, the International Finance Corporation (IFC), both of which recruit qualified professionals.

Other development finance institutions include the African Development Bank, which mobilises and allocates resources for investment in its regional member countries and provides policy advice and technical assistance to support development. The Bank is made up of three parts: the African Development Bank, the African Development Fund (ADF) and the Nigeria Trust Fund (NTF). With offices in 34 African countries, the bank recruits personnel for its head office in Abidjan and for its offices around the continent on fixed-term and permanent staffing contracts.

A number of United Nations agencies are also operational in Africa and, along with regional institutions such as ECOWAS and SADC, employ professionals with a range of backgrounds and expertise.

Professions on the Rise

As you consider your prospects within the African job market, you might well wonder which skills are particularly in demand in Africa today? The good news is that skills from pretty much every professional area can help you develop your career.

In the telecoms sector where mobile network operators generate the largest portion of revenue, opportunities for those with skills in mobile distribution and retail are available, as well as for application developers and content providers.

> *"Based on the requests we have for professionals, in southern Africa, I would say the key areas are Telecoms, Banking & Finance, Mining and Agriculture. In East Africa; Financial Services and Insurance, Agriculture, Health Services, Investment Vehicles and ICT. In West Africa; Oil & Gas, Agriculture, Financial Services and Health Services."*
>
> **Audrey Mensah, AMSCO**

Agriculture is a huge sector within the continent and one that is lacking in many of the skills needed. Studies conducted by the International Service for National Agricultural Research show a need for agricultural scientists, soil science specialist researchers and plant breeders. There are currently lower than required numbers of personnel in agricultural research, and all agricultural science disciplines are needed within the continent.

Professionals with skills across the range of professional services are also an attractive proposition for employers. Demand for accountancy services is expected to increase significantly in Africa with the adoption of international financial reporting standards (IFRS), and several countries are already experiencing severe skill shortages in this sector.

Skilled graduates and mid-level professionals with experience in non-financial professional services are also highly sought after in the governmental and public sectors, while shortages are acute at both technician and skilled professional levels in most countries.

There are also opportunities for middle-level professionals in legal services and outsourced legal processes from the West such as document editing and proofreading, litigation research, and intellectual property work, already provide career opportunities within African countries.

Global law firms are also increasingly interested in opportunities within the African market and a key factor for their continuing success will be their ability to hire talented lawyers into the region. 'Magic circle' firms such as Allan & Overy and Norton Rose have opened offices in Morocco, and Eversheds plans to expand its reach across the continent.

As large corporations and other investors ramp up their operations in Africa – a survey by market research group Acritas found that almost one-fifth of multinationals need lawyers in Africa outside South Africa – top law firms increasingly need lawyers in African countries to assist their clients to negotiate joint ventures, privatisations, exploration and project finance.

Although the scarcity of qualified legal practitioners in Africa is less severe than that of engineers or accountants, companies and law firms admit that there is a lack of qualified lawyers on the ground and often there can be a high attrition rate for those hired, as lawyers seek out the higher paid opportunities in sectors such as oil and shipping.

Engineers are also in high demand within African organisations. Civil engineers are a critical resource for the development and maintenance of physical infrastructure, while electrical engineers are needed to support the operation and management of utilities and other public networks. The demand by companies for engineering staff is expected to increase in Africa, creating many employment opportunities for qualified professionals.

Africa's cutting edge and innovative telecoms sector is a huge draw for ICT experts from outside the continent. Despite the sector's rapid development in recent years, there is still a significant digital divide between Africa and the rest of the world, giving rise to opportunities for those with the skills to bridge the gap. There are also opportunities for those with more traditional IT experience covering areas such as IT infrastructure development, installation, support, web design and software development.

The rapid development of the tourism sector in many African countries and the subsequent growth of their hospitality industries also bring significant employment opportunities in Africa for a range of jobs within the sector. From chefs to hospitality managers, the tourism industry is a key sector for jobs and countries such as South Africa have seen a rapid increase in employment within this area.

According to an April 2013 report from Statistics South Africa, there was a 10.2% increase in international tourist arrivals between 2011 and 2012, while in the previous year, employment in the tourism sector – as a percentage of overall employment in the country – rose 4.3 % to 4.5% – an increase of about 31,000 jobs. This trend creates hiring opportunities for those with experience in the food industry and the wine and beverage sector, as well as for those with experience in tourism, product development and photography.

The private sector has made inroads into many areas of public services. Examples include the growth in privately owned schools and hospitals that are keen to attract experienced education and health professionals.

The impact made by many private sector businesses in Africa has extended beyond their primary profit making agenda to include a raft of corporate social responsibility programmes geared towards improving public services,

> *"Professionals with skills and experience in technical or specialist disciplines are in higher demand e.g. engineering, telecoms, project management and health. This is to support the development of infrastructure, the increasing need for social connectedness, the growth in natural resources and health challenges. Demonstrated capability in business development, complemented with local knowledge, is also an asset that most businesses seek. Generally, opportunities are available in all disciplines, from graduate to executive level."*
>
> **Carol Hondonga, Rio Tinto**

health care, sanitation, water delivery, community relations and limiting environmental damage. As companies seek ways of improving the lives of their employees and the communities in which they operate, this has given rise to opportunities for professionals with expertise in CSR, stakeholder relations, supply chain management, corporate communications and corporate governance.

The public sector in many African countries has taken on the challenge of spearheading development programmes. As a result, the demand for managers with public policy making and service delivery skills and with the experience to manage diverse stakeholders from the private and public sectors on public policy issues is acute. Professionals with expertise in human resources management, finance, logistics and procurement management are also in high demand.

Don't forget that when you are researching who's hiring in Africa, your career opportunities are not limited to larger organisations. Most companies across the continent fall into the SME (small and medium sized enterprises) category, with fewer than 250 employees, and can offer attractive job roles and swift opportunities for advancement.

However, you will need to keep an open mind about what you can find, warns AMSCO executive, Audrey Mensah. "Many parts of Africa are still not advanced enough to embrace certain professions, so if you are in one of those very specialist professions – a paleontologist, for example! – you will need to get creative and make the skills you provide relevant in order to get hired."

You need to be able to translate the challenges and difficulties Africa faces into opportunities, insists Databank Group CEO, Keli Gadzekpo. "People should keep a very open mind and not get caught up in being a specialist, as the market place is wide open and still developing. The market may not be ready or interested in ideas that are too specialist, so people need to be good generalists and adapt to the opportunities. That's what I believe Africa has to offer; a diamond in the rough."

South Africa

If you are planning to enter the African job market, you should research data concerning employment and sector performance.

South Africa, for example, is in need of educated, qualified and experienced people with the right skills to help grow the country's economy.

In South Africa, despite high levels of unemployment, employers still struggle to fill vacancies that require technical skills and competencies. The Manpower Talent Shortage Survey released in May 2013, pointed out that engineers are still proving to be the most difficult position for companies to fill, followed by management and executive positions, teachers, legal staff and skilled trades.

This was followed by accounting and financial staff, restaurant and hotel staff, technicians, customer service representatives, customer support and IT staff. The survey also revealed that employers were finding it difficult to fill positions due to a lack of hard skills or technical competencies, and 30% of employers surveyed cited a lack of industry-specific qualifications or professional certifications.

The report identified in excess of 500,000 positions vacant in South Africa but there are insufficient trained and qualified people to fill these vacancies. South Africa has 1 engineer for every 3,200 people compared to 1 for every 130 in China, 250 in Europe and 450 in Australia. The South African government's list of scarce and critical skills shows that there is a shortage of 400,000 teachers in all subjects. In 2008 there was a shortage of 22,000 accounting specialists – 5,300 of whom should be chartered accountants. There are 70,000 positions available in Information Technology but only 17,000 learners have qualified over the last 10 years. There is a need for 30,000 registered nurses and 10,000 pharmacy assistants.

Another South African study, the Manpower Employment Outlook Survey (MEOS), found that the employers most likely to be recruiting were in the Agriculture, Hunting, Forestry and Fishing sectors and the Mining and Quarrying sector. Employers in other sectors such as electricity, gas and water supply and the finance, insurance, real estate and business services sectors were cautiously optimistic about hiring, while employers in the construction sector forecast negative hiring activity.

> *"Give to the world the best you have and the best will come back to you."*

Myrna Ericksen

Chapter 4

What Do I Bring to the Table?

While your main interest is in finding a great career opportunity with a great company, it's worth remembering that an organisation's only real interest is in understanding how hiring you will benefit their business. So, as you consider the sectors or industries on which you would like to focus your job search, it is important that you consider how you will market yourself to the companies that interest you.

'Selling' yourself isn't always an easy thing to do. Most of us are fairly modest about our skills and achievements and often don't even appreciate how much of what we know is of real value to someone else. Marketing yourself effectively to get the job you want will mean putting aside false modesty and looking objectively at what you have to offer.

The starting point for any successful sales campaign is to really know your product. When it comes to job hunting, *you* are the product and to be able to sell yourself successfully to an employer, you need to be clear about what you are bringing to the table in terms of skills, knowledge, motivation and experience.

> *"I would reject candidates unable to articulate how to handle the required activities and who come across as being interested only in what the organisation can provide, and not what they can bring to an organisation."*
>
> HR Manager, Zimbabwe

The '3 E's' and the '3 U's'

The great news is that, as we've seen, the African job market can offer you exciting career opportunities. Whether or not you are of African origin, there is a need for your skills in the diverse sectors and industries operating in the continent's emerging economies.

That said, while there are considerable benefits for employers in Africa in hiring people from outside the continent, there are some challenges in recruiting professionals from abroad, irrespective of their ethnicity. The benefits to employers are what I refer to as 'the 3 E's' and the challenges they face are what I will call 'the three U's'.

Let's start with the positives. The first 'E' is for experience. The experience that you have gathered from studying and working in developed markets is invaluable to employers in Africa, particularly if you have attended highly ranked educational institutions or worked for world-class organisations. The technical skills and discipline you will have acquired as a result of studying and working internationally is seen as a welcome advantage to their organisations.

The second 'E' stands for exposure. Your exposure to other cultures and professional working practices as a result of living and working outside Africa is another positive for employers who are seeking to introduce diversity and internationally competitive standards into their businesses.

The third 'E' denotes excellence. While there is no guarantee of anyone's performance just because they have been working in more developed markets, there is an assumption that working abroad gives you highly rated skills and expertise, particularly when your skills may be in short supply locally.

The not so good news is that employers in Africa can be put off by negative perceptions of external hires, and sometimes for good reason – as illustrated by 'the 3 U's'.

The first 'U' stands for 'uncommitted' and refers to the fact that there will be those who are recruited into one organisation but will be constantly on the lookout for reasons to move on to another company, or even return to the country they left. Companies invest time, money and business relationships in their recruitment process and are loath, quite understandably, to recruit people who don't appear to be adaptable or to have staying power.

The second 'U' stands for unrealistic. Whether it's the salary on offer for a job, the living conditions within a particular area or country, the lifestyle afforded by the job or the level of job on offer, one of the major complaints that companies have about those wanting to move to Africa is that they are unrealistic in their expectations.

The third 'U' is for uninformed. Despite my many years of work as a career coach, I am still surprised by how little research some people will undertake before applying for a job, even when it involves making major decisions such as moving to another country.

Job applicants who have little or no knowledge about a company, let alone about a country and its culture and customs, are unlikely to be attractive candidates for companies who are looking for talent for their business. Even if you have a link to a particular country by birth or heritage, it's not enough to assume that you will be seen as a credible candidate if you don't come prepared.

> *"The job market in Africa is more sophisticated than some people think. The people who have skills have surprisingly good choices, due to the proliferation of NGOs, bilateral organisations and access to funds. But you can't assume that because you possess sought after skills, you will automatically get a job. There is real competition for those jobs."*
>
> **Bernie Akporiaye, Senegal**

Summarising My Personal Strengths

If you are interested in working in Africa, what then are the things that you should be doing to underscore the positive perceptions of 'the 3 E's' and to overcome the negative '3 U's'?

First of all, you have to be clear about exactly what you can offer a company before you are able to 'sell yourself' effectively. Most of us do our jobs without spending too much time analysing what we are good at and where we excel. We might acknowledge that there are parts of our jobs that are a bit more of a struggle than others, but unless we're required to do it for an interview or an appraisal, it's likely that we haven't had to assess our skills and expertise in any real depth.

Although it can be an uncomfortable experience to evaluate yourself critically, this is the time to really take stock of your strengths and weaknesses so that you can be clear about what you bring to the table. This will not only help you focus more clearly on identifying the right type of job, it will also help you market yourself more effectively, both in your CV and at interviews.

As a starting point, identify the specific skills that you have acquired both from your education and the jobs you've done or are doing. Your skills might include budgeting, financial management, recruiting, negotiating, IT programming, team leadership or problem solving, for example.

If you are struggling to identify your skills, ask your colleagues or friends what they think your strengths are and be open to what they tell you.

Some of your skills may be directly relevant to the job role you have in mind for the African job market, while others may be skills that you have developed and which could be transferred into a new sector or job role. When you think about skills and experience, consider the totality of your skills and how you acquired them, rather than the specific type of job that you do or have done.

One approach you can take to analysing your skills is to list them as if you were making an inventory of everything that you are able to do. Some of these may be skills you use frequently in your current job, others may be skills that you only make use of occasionally.

To make it simpler, break your inventory down into skills that relate to the following 4 key areas:

- People
- Information
- Ideas
- Professional/Technical.

Having listed every skill you can think of under each of these headings, take a moment to consider which you enjoy using and why. While we may be good at some skills, these are not necessarily the ones we enjoy using. Alternatively, we may enjoy doing some things but not be particularly skilful at doing them. An analysis of your skills in this way will help remind you of what you do well and what you enjoy, but might need to improve upon.

Use a scoring system of 1 to 4 to rate each skill. First, rate each skill you have identified based on how competent you are in your ability to use this skill (on a scale of 1 for basic level of competency to 4 for highly skilful). Then rate each skill according to how much you enjoy using it (1 for least level of enjoyment to 4 for most).

This analysis will help you assess whether you have the skills required for a particular job role or if there are gaps in your knowledge or expertise. It will also remind you of what you do best and enjoy most, both aspects being critical to how effective and successful you will be in a job. Also, as you think about how you acquired your skills, it will remind you of achievements that you can refer to in your CV or during any interviews.

However, as we know, the ability to do a good job is not based solely on your skills, but also on how you are required to do the job and the environment or working culture in which you are expected to do it.

> *"Your international experience and skills are required and valued. Show confidence without arrogance. Living and working in Africa will be different; challenging but extremely fulfilling as your career progresses."*
>
> **Carol Hondonga, Rio Tinto**

Knowing your product – you – also involves understanding your values and what really drives you when it comes to your career. This requires you to be totally honest about yourself, your skills, your personality and your motivations.

One way of thinking about your work values might be to consider which aspects of your job that you find the most satisfying. For example, it might be the areas of your job that relate to helping other people, such as training or coaching colleagues or subordinates.

Thinking through how you like to work – your preferred style of working – is also important. We all have different personalities; some of us like working under pressure in a fast-moving environment; others prefer to have a clear idea of what is expected of them and then be left to get on with it. Some people like team working, while others prefer to work independently.

The type of organisation that you think you would be most effective in is also an important consideration. Do you work more effectively within a structured organisation with clearly defined roles or do you find yourself better able to deliver within a flatter, more creative or dynamic culture? Are you attracted to large organisations with a known brand or is your preference for smaller organisations with a more flexible way of working and where you can make your mark more quickly?

The one thing you can be sure of is that the working environment in Africa will be different to what you are used to, making it crucial that you know yourself and what it takes for you to thrive.

Assessing My Value to an Organisation

The most effective way to sell any product is to demonstrate the benefits of that product to the buyer. In thinking about your value to an organisation, you should be aware not only of what your skills are, but how those skills will make a positive difference to the organisation's ability to achieve its objectives.

Let's imagine that your job is to sell shampoo. Any brand of shampoo can be used to wash hair so if you are to be an effective salesperson, you will need to convince your customers that your brand of shampoo is better than other brands and that they would benefit in some way from buying from you. You could explain, for example, how your brand of shampoo leaves hair feeling silkier than other brands or demonstrate that it promotes faster hair growth, or even point out that your shampoo is much less expensive than comparable products, making it more affordable for your buyer.

The key point is that, as a good salesperson, the onus is on you to know your product and to figure out which benefits will be of interest to your customer. After all, how many bottles of shampoo do you think you would sell if you couldn't tell your customers why they should buy it, or if you told them to read all the ingredients listed on the bottle and decide for themselves if it was a product that they could use?

If you have completed your skills inventory, you should be clear about what you have to offer an organisation and what you bring to the table. Your goal now is to articulate this in a way that highlights the benefits to them of hiring you.

Knowing your product – yourself – is one part of this. The other part of the equation is a detailed knowledge of your potential buyer and what they are looking for. Once you are clear about this from your research, it's then a matter of putting the two things together to create an irresistible package – you!

Think carefully about who needs your skills. An organisation in the not-for-profit sector might value your fundraising skills, for example, while a company that markets high profile brands may want your skills in marketing and public relations. Alternatively, you could be a valuable asset to a growing SME if you have proven business development skills.

You can better assess how useful you can be to an organisation when you understand what their goals are and which of your skills will help to achieve them.

Transferring My Skills to another Sector

It might be the case that you see a move to work in Africa as a chance to change your career direction in some way.

Perhaps the kind of work you have been doing is very specific to the country in which you live and is not readily available within the African job market. It could also be the case that you have been working in a sector or job role that doesn't reflect your education and qualifications or that simply no longer interests you.

Whatever the reason, if you are planning to change your career path or sector, it is even more important that you focus on identifying the skills that you have acquired. It is these skills that you want to persuade an employer that you can transfer and adapt successfully to their industry and activities.

Part of your strategy will involve creating a CV that focuses more on your skills than on the specific nature of the job roles that you have undertaken in the past. This helps to take the focus off your industry/sector experience and to emphasise the type of skills you have developed, rather than the specific context in which you used those skills in the past.

Changing sector or job role will also require you to think about how your skills can be 'translated' into the sector or job role you are now interested in. The following is an example of how you can do this.

Case Study

Henry, aged 35, has worked for ten years in local government in the UK. His most recent experience has included several years as a Project Manager in the Housing department of his local municipality. This involved working extensively in the social housing area, dealing with tenants within a number of local authorities and resolving their issues. He has worked closely with rent and housing benefit departments and sourced and set up agreements with maintenance contractors.

Henry is keen to move his career to Africa and realises that he is unlikely to find another role dealing with social housing, as this does not exist in the African country he has in mind.

His preference is to move into the private sector and to find a role with a large corporation. Having assessed his skills, he realises that his greatest strengths lie in community engagement, strategy development, conflict resolution, procurement and project management. He also has a good knowledge of two of the languages spoken in the country he has in mind.

With some career coaching, he is able to redefine a new career direction and is now clear that his skills and experience can be used to target a role that involves assisting a large corporation in the African country of his choice with developing and implementing corporate funded community based programmes and corporate social responsibility projects.

Going through this exercise has helped Henry to set out a clear direction for what he wants to do and he can now adapt his strategy for 'selling' himself towards identifying and targeting a company that would be likely to employ someone in this kind of role.

> *"Research what the needs and gaps are in the country you want to go into so that you are a desirable candidate. This will put you in a strong negotiating position to get the attractive package that you are looking for."*
>
> Elvina Quaison, Ghana

> *"Plans are only good intentions unless they immediately degenerate into hard work."*

Peter Drucker

Chapter 5

What's my Career Strategy?

If you want to achieve your goal of moving your career to Africa, it will entail some hard work. Even the best strategy doesn't implement itself, and all your plans will mean nothing unless you are committed to doing the work that is necessary to succeed.

Treat your job search like a project. Like any project, you will need to have a strategy to help you focus on your objective and to keep yourself on track. As business author Henry Mintzberg says, "Strategy is not the consequence of planning, but the opposite: its starting point."

There are two steps to this process. The first is to think about the kind of role that makes sense in terms of where you see your career developing. Could this mean a more senior role, or one at the same level but giving you greater exposure to new projects and the opportunity to learn new skills? Or, is it time for a change of career, industry or sector? Is your next step to find a similar job in a different market or are you ready for a more senior role in an emerging market?

Once you are clear on the first step, the second step to consider is your job search strategy. Finding a job will involve undertaking detailed research on the country you are interested in, the sector or industries you want to target and the type of job roles that you would like to get. It will involve building and extending your network, identifying the different routes into the African job market and making judicious use of the social media tools available to you.

You've probably heard it said that failing to plan is planning to fail, so once you've clarified your strategy, it's time to develop a plan and put it into action.

Researching Opportunities

It's almost impossible to overstate the importance of research as you consider your move to Africa. As we've seen, there are many myths and misconceptions about the continent and what it offers, which means that you really have to do your homework.

There has been such rapid change in many African countries that even if you are targeting a job role in your country of origin, you need to bear in mind that many things may have changed since you left, or even last visited.

Paul Kasimu, a Human Resources Director for Diageo in East Africa, advises Africans returning to the continent to stay abreast of developments there.

"Africans should not simply say I want to go back to a particular country but not know what exists there," he says. "There can be a huge disconnect between people's aspirations and the realities on the ground. My advice is that Africans outside need to match their training and expertise to what pertains. Their specific skills or functions may not be relevant to the home market, so they need to look at their transferable skills and match these to the roles that are relevant to the market they are targeting."

If you are not of African origin or don't yet know much about the continent, remember that the sheer size and diversity of Africa is such that you need to do your homework about the specific country or countries that you have in mind. Being informed is a key part of your strategy and this includes regularly reading up on the business, social and political developments taking place in the country.

Doing your research also means researching the business areas and the companies that are hiring and making use of any information that you pick up. For example, a new oil and gas find in a particular country could be a good indicator that the companies involved in the find might be looking to hire more people. Similarly, a press article about a company's expansion programme into Africa might suggest opportunities for your skills and experience.

You should also research areas such as:

- Government and country specific websites for information about the country, the economy, the climate, and any work-related legislation and work permit conditions

- Corporate websites for background information about target companies and organisations, including their services or business lines, clients, corporate culture and job opportunities

- Trends and activities within your sector of interest, including the key players and the major issues that the sector is facing

- Recruitment companies and headhunters that cover the country or region

- Professional organisations and associations related to your profession within the country or region, or which operate globally

- Key information about the country relevant to your personal situation, e.g. medical facilities, accommodation costs, immigration requirements, shipping agents, schools, rules on dependents, transportation, and the cost of living.

The best type of research, though, is what can be done in person and you should plan a visit to the country you would like to work in to really get a feel for what living there would be like. Going in person is also a great opportunity to make new contacts and to visit some potential target companies.

If you are planning a trip, try to avoid Christmas and other major holiday periods as key people are likely to be away and it's harder to get a real sense of the country as it normally operates.

Elvina Quaison, who moved to Ghana from the UK, is a strong advocate of taking a preliminary trip. "Plan to be in your country of choice for two to three months to find a job as many employers will want to meet you and see you in country before they take your interest seriously."

Making a visit is essential, agrees Audrey Mensah, who recruits senior executives through management services company, AMSCO.

"Once you have determined the country in which you wish to work, whether it's your home country or not, you need to visit, meet and speak with as many people as you can, and establish contact with relevant agencies that can assist you in your search," she says. She encourages job seekers to keep an open mind and to also explore opportunities for consultancies and short-term contracts.

"You should remain completely open to all options and not only target multinationals, but also purely local companies with great potential to grow in their own space."

If a trip isn't possible, at the very least the internet provides access to a wide range of information as well as news and business websites that you can access to help with your research.

"Give yourself enough time to find a job," Audrey warns. "If you are already in a good job, don't give that up in the belief that you will find something suitable in Africa immediately. You may need to give it up at a later stage and be in-country to assess the opportunities that may be coming up. Another option is to work as a Consultant in the interim while you carry on your job search."

> *"If I could change anything, it would have been to do my research on all aspects of my move; the cost of living, social networks, and the culture and ways of thinking about things, even personal space. This is really important and cultural sensitivity is key – especially if you assume that because you are of African origin, you know how it works!"*
>
> **Ernestina Boadi on her move to Ghana**

Building an Effective Network

No matter where in the world you are, your networks and contacts are incredibly important. In Africa, where there is a general acceptance of the principle of mutual help and support, it is very often a case of whom you know and who they, in turn, also know.

Whether you have to deal with minor inconveniences or resolve major problems, having a strong network can make all the difference. Creating and making the right contacts in the country you are targeting can save you time, aggravation and disappointment, while having the wrong people in your environment can leave you disheartened and ready to return.

We hear a lot about the importance of networking today and while the concept is nothing new, its application to our business relationships has become much more important, particularly where opportunities may be more difficult to access. Other people are often the best source of information, and networking effectively is less about just adding to your contacts on LinkedIn or Facebook, and more about building strategic relationships.

Many jobs in Africa are not formally advertised, so restricting your search to jobs advertised online or in publications will not be enough. A key part of your strategy has to include making use of your contacts and network, both online and face-to-face, to find out more about the companies you are interested in. Networking effectively means talking to people, engaging with potential employers and building relationships so that you come to mind as and when opportunities arise.

Effective networking brings a number of benefits and, when it comes to searching for a job, it is one of the best ways to identify opportunities and connect with relevant recruiters. Even if the people in your network can't directly offer you a job, they can help you with advice or information and can refer you to those who are in a position to hire you. Networking is also an effective route to jobs that are less likely to be advertised, particularly if you are a specialist or at a very senior level.

What defines your network? Everyone you know is effectively part of your network: friends, family, ex-colleagues, alumni, college professors, church members, social contacts, and so on. If you have any part of your network in Africa already, this is the time to revive dormant contacts, reconnect with those you know and let people know what your plans are and how they can help you. Your network in Africa will help to give you a realistic picture of what working there is like and can steer you towards their contacts and advise you on the right approach to adopt.

The ability to network effectively will be an important part of your job search strategy because it's important to remember that personal endorsements can make a big difference. When recruiters are looking for candidates, they will look more favourably on a qualified candidate who is referred to them, and even more so if the person doing the referring is someone they know and trust. Having someone introduce you to a recruiter can greatly increase your chances as you benefit from the strength of your referrer's reputation.

> *"I went about my job search through family, personal contacts and advertised vacancies. I started e-mailing and calling everyone I knew in Nigeria six months in advance. I had to be tenacious, though, and my imminent move finally started to register with them about three months later. But it wasn't until I was actually there, on the ground, that they believed me!"*
>
> **Simi Belo on her move to Nigeria**

Even a referral from someone who may not personally know you will help your chances, as the recruiter is likely to be impressed by that person staking their credibility on you. A number of companies make use of internal referral systems to identify new hires, which means that the better your network, the easier it will be to connect to people within companies who can help to get you an interview.

Be mindful that the person endorsing you is putting themselves on the line by doing so, and that how you behave will also impact on their reputation. This puts the onus on you to take the referral seriously and be well prepared to give substance to their recommendation. It's also a good idea to let the person who referred you know what happened as a result of their input. They will appreciate the courtesy and are more likely to refer you again and help you extend your network further.

You can improve the effectiveness of your networking by:

- **Being clear about what you want to achieve through your network.** While your ultimate goal is to get a job, most of your contacts are not in a position to offer you one and you therefore need to identify what you want from the contacts you approach.

- **Having a clear message about the job you want.** Your network of contacts can't help you if they are not sure what kind of role you are looking for and the experience you bring. By giving them a simple and clear message of the kind of job/company/industry you are targeting, they will be better placed to connect you to the right people within their own networks.

- **Being clear about why you are approaching someone**. Let the network contact know what you want from them; it could me a phone conversation about the industry you are interested in, a brief meeting to get their insights on a company they know well, or an introduction to someone that you are trying to meet. Let people know how you got their details and what steps you will take with the information they give you.

- **Planning how you will contact referrals.** Decide on whether it's more appropriate to phone, send an e-mail or go for a face to face meeting. Be ready to open the conversation with your reasons for contacting them and check that it's a convenient time for them to hear from you.

- **Starting networking with people you know.** Your friends and family are a good starting point for extending your network as they already know and trust you. Be open about asking for help – just as you would be willing to help a friend, your personal network will also want to help you.

- **Avoiding putting pressure on your network**. Particularly when it comes to family and friends, be careful that you are not trying to push them into doing something that makes them uncomfortable even though they want to help you.

- **Sharing the results.** Let your network contacts know the outcome of their referrals. It's not only courteous, but it will also let them know how useful their own contacts are, and prompt them to offer further contacts or suggestions.

- **Maintaining voice communication.** Don't stop talking – e-mails and social media posts are great ways of contacting people, but talking is always the most effective way of communicating and it helps to avoid any misunderstandings in content and tone, which can sometimes happen with electronic communication.

Following up with contacts you have met is one of the most important elements of effective networking. Holding onto business cards and neglecting introduction e-mails suggests that you are not serious about finding a role. Following up on an initial conversation or introduction will help you develop the relationship and build on a positive first impression.

A key point to remember is that networking is a long-term career strategy, and that building and maintaining a great network takes time and effort. It's less about quantity and more about the quality of your contacts, and sustaining genuine and meaningful relationships requires you to show interest in your contacts and not just see them as a source of help for you. Offering something to people in your network helps to build goodwill and makes them more inclined to assist you, should the need arise.

> *"Given what I know now, I would have done a better job of networking before I came to Africa."*
>
> **Bernie Akporiaye**

Routes to the African Job Market

Your job search strategy should include a plan for approaching jobs through a variety of routes. One way to think of accessing the job market is to imagine an iceberg – part of it is visible above the water but the greater part is hidden below.

The visible routes to the job market are the obvious ones of recruitment agencies, jobs boards, and online and print media. The invisible or 'hidden' job market is everything else that gives you indirect access to jobs and recruiters.

The visible route includes jobs that are publicly advertised. These might be advertised by companies on their own websites, through online job boards or in the press, or in specialised media and their associated websites. Some professional associations also publish job vacancies on their websites, although in some cases these are only accessible to their members.

There are an increasing number of recruiters and online jobs boards that cover jobs in Africa and you can research those that focus on your sector or country of interest and that carry the level and type of jobs that you are looking for.

Your research should also have helped you identify the kind of companies and organisations that you are interested in and you can create a list of targeted companies and register on their recruitment sites, setting up alerts for new jobs that come up.

Online job searches can be time consuming and dispiriting, particularly when you receive no feedback from your applications. You will need to be persistent and to ensure that your application closely reflects the requirements of the job.

> *"Keep up to date and research the sectors to identify target companies. Then get to know those companies and use social networks to connect with people working in those companies or who know people there."*
>
> **Carol Hondonga, Rio Tinto**

The hidden job market offers you alternative routes to get to job opportunities and decision makers. These routes include:

- **Direct approaches to companies**. A direct approach to a company or organisation can occasionally yield results if you are clear about what the company does and how your skills and experience could be of value. Most companies appreciate the opportunity to save on recruitment agency commissions and recruitment advertising fees, while some actually incentivise their employees to find candidates for internal vacancies. With this approach, you need to research who would be receptive to seeing your CV and have a good understanding of the company's business and the issues or problems that your skills are able to help them solve. Find a name or contact to approach and make sure that your application is tailored towards that specific organisation, keeping it short and easy to read. Follow up by phone and try to set up an informal meeting or discussion to find out more about internal possibilities now or in the near future.

- **School/University Alumni.** However long it is since you left your school or University, chances are that you can still tap into the alumni network. Alumni offices can help with identifying alumni within your target companies, and making contact with them will give you the chance to find out more about the company, obtain the names of relevant contacts to approach and learn about internal opportunities in their organisations.

- **Careers & Job Fairs**. There are a number of careers and job fairs related to working in Africa. This route has the advantage of giving you the opportunity to make direct contact with companies and organisations recruiting in Africa without having to travel very far. By speaking to representatives of the company, you can find out more about their hiring needs and might even obtain an interview on the spot. The disadvantage of this route is that some careers fairs will screen CVs in advance and only set up interviews with pre-selected candidates, making it more difficult to access the opportunity if the deadline has passed. Some can also get quite crowded, making meaningful interaction and discussion with companies – particularly those with big brand names – quite difficult.

- **Events and Conferences**. Conferences and events related to Africa are a useful way to network and gain access to influential contacts in your sector. By approaching senior executives who speak at conferences, you can make valuable business contacts that can connect you to opportunities within their company or their network. Prepare for events by identifying who you would like to meet and how you plan to approach them, and be sure to take business cards and exchange them with new contacts.

- **Professional Associations**. Recruiters seeking candidates from particular professions often advertise on niche professional sites or in publications where they are more likely to identify candidates for specialist vacancies. Researching the national professional associations and bodies within the country you are interested in will give you insights into the key issues for the profession in that country and information about potential employers.

- **African Professional Networks**. There is a wide range of networks bringing together African professionals abroad and, if you don't have any immediate contacts with a connection to Africa, these are a good place to start making some. Some network groups are focused on particular countries, while others have members from specific professions or sectors.

Keep organised and on track with all your approaches. You can manage this process using a simple spreadsheet that you can set up to record the job sites you need to visit regularly, jobs you have applied for, contacts you have approached, and any action required.

Peter Ndegwa of the global drinks group, Diageo, encourages a mix of approaches when it comes to his company.

"For people interested in working with us, I would say that you should go to events that Diageo is involved with and take the opportunity to meet our business leaders ad HR representatives, or our partners who focus on Africa and can connect you to the company. For those who come on holiday, get in touch; we are very receptive and happy to consider CVs that come through."

> *"You need to be tenacious with your contacts in Africa. I am not being patronising when I say that they do not have the same views towards time and promise keeping as in the West, and they actually rely on your persistence."*
>
> **Simi Belo, Nigeria**

The Pluses and Pitfalls of Social Media

An increasingly critical route to the hidden job market is through the effective use of social media and you should make online networking a key part of your job search strategy. While this route offers many benefits, you need to manage your online presence to make sure that it supports rather than sabotages your search.

Social media, and LinkedIn in particular, provide a route to potential recruiters by helping you to bypass the gatekeepers that stand between you and the chance to pitch for a job. For example, LinkedIn can help you find the business manager or human resources executive of the company you want to approach and then present yourself directly as a candidate.

While there are a growing number of new social media platforms, most people look to Facebook, Twitter and LinkedIn as their first ports of call. Facebook and Twitter tend to be used for more social interaction, while LinkedIn has rapidly become the platform of choice for professionals.

As at October 2013, LinkedIn had over 238 million users worldwide, with two new members joining per second, and 10 million members in Africa. According to the company, 81% of companies use LinkedIn to recruit, making it a platform that you can't afford to ignore when it comes to job hunting.

Having a good LinkedIn profile that clearly sets out your skills and experience is now a standard requirement for any job seeker. Recruiters search periodically to find relevant profiles and are able to target very specific candidates based on the information in their job profiles. Recruiters can also use a variety of online recruitment tools, pay-per-click campaigns and search engine optimisation to target key words, qualifications, and phrases describing a position. As these tools channel only relevant search results, it is important that your profile is targeted towards the sector and job type you want, making it is easy for them to find you.

Building a network of the right kind of contacts for your industry sector or profession on LinkedIn will give you a virtual address book that you can leverage to connect you to the right people. While you can search for people and companies yourself, requesting an introduction from someone you know can be more effective than a cold introduction that you have to initiate.

A great network includes people you know who can vouch for your abilities and performance and who are willing to recommend you to others. To use LinkedIn effectively, you have to be proactive and prepared to ask for what you need. Ask your contacts if they can recommend you to people they know who are connected to companies or industries of interest, or can send them an e-mail to introduce you. If there is a particular job you are interested in, you can use LinkedIn to find out who you are connected to that knows someone in that company and can refer you.

You can increase your visibility by joining or starting a LinkedIn group. There are more than 600 groups focused on emerging markets, for example, and being part of a group of like minded professionals posing questions and contributing to the dialogue is a great way to enhance your credibility. Jobs relating to a group are frequently advertised on group discussions, making it easier for you to find out about relevant employment opportunities.

For all the pluses that social media offers, it also has its pitfalls and you do need to be very careful about your online presence.

Employers are people too, and are just as social-media savvy as the people they are looking to hire. Whether or not you think it's intrusive, employers and recruiters are increasingly using technology to scan your online reputation as part of their hiring process, and surveys of industry executives have shown that a candidate's social media profile has caused them not to hire that person.

A would-be employer looking at a potential recruit's profile on social networking websites such as Facebook and Twitter is looking for clues into the real you, and if your digital footprint is unprofessional, you could potentially unravel all the benefits of a great CV and network.

Your social media profile is a powerful way to open up job opportunities, but it must be managed in a responsible way. Think of your online footprint as an important part of your personal brand, and when you are writing your profile or posting status updates, threads and pictures, be aware of how these might influence a potential employer's decision to hire you.

Using Recruiters and Headhunters

A key partner in your job search will be professional recruiters and headhunters as many companies prefer to outsource their recruitment needs to these professionals. There are a number of international recruitment agencies that hire on behalf on clients in Africa. While some specialise in sectors such as Oil & Gas or Finance, others recruit across a broader portfolio of sectors and jobs.

There will also be recruitment consultancies in the African country you are targeting and you can research these through online searches, through information portals like ReConnect Africa.com, and by talking to friends and contacts in your network. Check the websites of the agencies you hear about and see which organisations they recruit for and the level and types of jobs into which they place their candidates.

Good recruiters can provide you with invaluable access to companies and to information about salary levels and compensation in their particular markets. They will also be able to advise you on the skills and expertise in demand within their local markets and help you adapt your CV, if necessary, to meet the particular demands of their clients. Good recruiters with strong client relationships can also help to create opportunities on your behalf by positioning you favourably towards the skills gaps they know that their client companies need to fill.

You can help a recruiter to help you by providing them with a clear picture of what you are looking for and the key skills that you offer to an employer. The more specific you can be about your sector/industry of interest, the location and type of role that interests you, the better they can help to place you.

Recruiters are paid when they place candidates, so keep in mind that a recruiter's key priority is to fill a vacancy and not to search for a role on your behalf. They are an important element in your job search but you should never rely solely on agencies to find you work.

You need to manage your relationships with recruitment agencies and you can do this by:

- **Being clear about your needs**. Treat your recruiter as your career ambassador and be upfront about your plans; when you intend to make the move, the kind of role you are interested in, what support you will need to make a decision, and so on.

- **Being selective about choosing the right agencies**. Find out whether they are among the preferred recruiters for particular firms or specialise in a particular sector. Ask your network contacts if they can give you any feedback on them.

- **Building a good long-term relationship with your recruitment consultant**. If possible, meet up with them so you can get a better idea of their capabilities and they can better understand how to market you.

- **Keeping track of your CV**. Insist on knowing where your CV is being sent, and to whom. This avoids duplication between competing recruiters and also helps you manage your own networking efforts.

- **Staying in touch**. Keep in regular contact with your recruiter but do bear in mind that they may also face delays and difficulties in dealing with client companies and may not always be able to act as quickly as you would like. Stay on good terms when you find a role as you may need their services again in the future.

For senior executive or specialist vacancies, companies frequently turn to executive search firms, or headhunters, to identify candidates. Headhunters might work on contingency – searching for people for roles and receiving payment only when they make a successful placement – or on a retained basis. If they have been retained by a corporate client, headhunters receive part of their payment for the search, whether or not they make a placement, and the rest of the payment once a candidate has been hired.

Depending on the level of seniority, specialism or sensitivity involved, some of the jobs that headhunters take on will not be openly advertised. Good headhunters are very familiar with a particular market and will use their personal networks as well as professional researchers to reach out to potential candidates, based on the brief they have been given by their client. An initial contact from a headhunter may be made confidentially by telephone, e-mail or through LinkedIn, with a follow up meeting arranged if you are interested in learning more.

To make your profile one that attracts headhunters, you need to have your profile and CV on a social networking site like LinkedIn and make sure that it contains the relevant key words and skills. Your level of visibility will also be enhanced through speaking engagements at conferences, contributions to discussion forums and publishing thought leadership articles relating to your sector.

The support of a good headhunter is an invaluable asset during your job search as they can help you to really understand an organisation and can negotiate a job offer and package with you.

If you believe a headhunter would be interested in your profile, research relevant headhunters and talk to your contacts to see if they have any experience of headhunters or know of one they could recommend.

> *"The only person who can pull me down is myself, and I'm not going to let myself pull me down anymore."*
>
> C. JoyBell C.

Chapter 6

How Do I Sell Myself?

On of the biggest complaints voiced by recruiters is the mismatch between the expectations of employers and the performance of candidates – particularly younger candidates – at the recruitment stage.

Employers frequently complain about poorly written CVs and a lack of preparation by candidates who are unable to 'sell themselves' positively and instead show a general lack of understanding of how to present themselves, a poor knowledge of the company they are approaching and the expectations of the job.

Why does this happen? Sometimes the lack of preparation can be put down to candidates not taking the process seriously or thinking that they can simply 'wing' the interview process. Sometimes, though, it's because people find it tough to position themselves favourably. As we saw in an earlier chapter, analysing our skills and knowing what we bring to the table can be a difficult exercise. Quite often we don't see ourselves in the same way that others see us and we can underestimate our abilities and undersell our achievements. We might also have some mental blocks about our abilities or negative beliefs about ourselves.

It's important to keep your motivation for working in Africa in mind and not to let yourself feel daunted about taking on a role that will challenge you. How you see yourself will come across to a recruiter or at interview. In order to sell yourself effectively, take the time to acknowledge any negative self-beliefs that can block your ability to position yourself as the ideal candidate for the job of your choice.

Pitching My Brand

If you've completed your skills inventory (*see Chapter 4*), you will have a good idea of your technical, people, ideas and information skills. You will also have thought about how to transfer these skills into another organisation or sector or even onto a completely different career path.

So now the question is whether you can convince a potential employer that you fit their bill? Can you 'pitch' yourself so that you appear to be the best candidate for the job and for their organisation?

People who are setting up a new business are often advised to have an elevator pitch i.e. a short statement that quickly tells someone about their business, the benefits it offers and what makes it special. Entrepreneurs are also encouraged to identify a 'USP' – unique selling point – that sets their product or service apart.

You can use your skills inventory to help you to develop an elevator pitch to potential employers about yourself and to identify your unique selling points. Your pitch should answer the following questions:

- Why should an organisation hire you?

- What value will you bring to the business?

- How will you be able to make a difference as a result?

- What evidence is there from your previous jobs or education to support this?

There are a few steps that you can take to help you develop your pitch.

1. Make a list of your achievements

Think of some of the things that you have achieved so far, whether as part of your current or previous jobs or during your education. Think of specific things you have done which made a positive impact and which brought you satisfaction. Even if you achieved something as part of a team, what was your personal contribution? Be as specific as possible and explain the outcome and impact that made it an achievement. For example:

- Led a team of analysts responsible for developing a new cash flow model, resulting in significant cost savings for a major client

- Developed a new database which enabled the IT Support team to track progress with client support tickets and improve resolution times

- Managed a major fundraising project from conception to implementation, bringing on board 3 new sponsors

- Identified new suppliers and negotiated improved rates for the business, resulting in a 20% reduction in input costs

These achievements will remind you of the value you have brought to previous organisations, some of which could be applicable to the organisations you now want to approach.

2. Write a personal profile

Think about how you want to be perceived and what you want to do and write a short profile that summarises you in that way. Your profile should briefly cover what you have done, your key skills and what you can do. An example of a profile is:

'I am a qualified accountant and project manager with 8 years experience of working within the oil and gas sector. I have led project teams on a range of business transformation initiatives and successfully managed budgets of up to £20 million. My key strengths lie in assessing project risks within this sector and successfully leading diverse teams to implement change within pre-set budgets.'

3. Then answer the following:

- **What type of role/position do I want?**

Try and be as specific as you can about the type of job role you are seeking. Avoid thinking in generalities – e.g. 'a management role in banking'.

- **What are my skills – directly applicable and transferable?**

Practice summarising your personal strengths. Recognise your strengths/USPs and how you have applied them in the past.

- **What does the market I'm targeting want?**

Your research, as well as your discussions with your network and recruiters, should give you insights into the types of skills and opportunities available.

- **What is my pitch to this market?**

Bring together your profile, your skills, your achievements and the needs of the market you are targeting to develop your pitch. Linking what you offer with what your target market needs creates the perfect pitch for the job you want.

> *"Position your skills and expertise for the African market. By knowing the local context, reflect on how you can add value and articulate that."*
>
> **Carol Hondonga, Rio Tinto**

Creating a Winning CV

Writing the perfect CV to win you an interview and a job offer will take thought and planning. A CV is generally the first impression a potential employer will get of you and, as with any first impression, it's important to make sure that it is a positive one.

It's fair to say that most recruiters spend very little time reading a CV, typically less than three minutes, and will quickly move on to the next one if they don't immediately see what they are looking for in a candidate. For this reason 'generic' CVs that don't immediately relate to the job role are usually consigned to the bin as recruiters will not take the time to wade through lots of information and try to figure out your skills and capabilities.

As Audrey Mensah of AMSCO explains, "I would reject an application for a number of reasons. For instance, if the candidate failed to adhere to the requirements stated in the advert, if the CV has typographical errors, if the applicant has attached a generic application letter which has no relevance to the job for which they are applying, if the CV is too long and the information is predominantly about subjects studied at school and all the short courses they have ever attended, whether relevant or not."

When it comes to applying for work in another country, don't make assumptions about the information on your CV. Don't assume, for example, that people have heard of your current employer and know what they do, or that in-house job titles will mean something to someone outside that organisation. Avoid including details or making reference to specific expertise that would not be needed in the country to which you are applying for work.

While there is no science to writing a CV – and there will be some variations in what people in different countries might expect to see in the document – there are some accepted principles that would apply to most recruiters and employers in Africa when it comes to a CV.

Your CV is fundamentally a document designed to sell your skills and experience to an employer and to persuade them to interview you. For this reason, a winning CV has to be one that focuses on the skills and expertise that matters to the potential employer and not simply lists all the jobs and job responsibilities you have held in the past.

A powerful CV will give the recruiter information about the key skills you have that relate to the job they want to fill and how you have applied these skills to good effect in your current and past roles. A high impact CV will succinctly highlight your relevant qualifications, your areas of strength and your key achievements.

> *"A CV is attractive when it is easy on the eye, has no unnecessary fanciful fonts, and has captured relevant information so that, at a glance, the skills and competencies of the applicant are evident."*
>
> **Audrey Mensah, AMSCO**

You should use your CV to show the best of your achievements, but make sure that what you state is both true and believable. According to Keli Gadzekpo of Databank Group, what he looks for in a CV are practical capabilities and he would reject a CV that listed "lofty achievements that seem contrived, or short stints on several jobs."

Although some CVs may end up longer or shorter, it is generally seen as good practice to keep your CV to a maximum of two pages. There are a number of approaches to presenting a CV and, depending on what you are trying to achieve, some of them are more effective than others. Broadly speaking, the following are some of the approaches you can take to crafting your CV:

- **Chronological CV.** This is the format used in most cases and is effective when applying for a role that leads on logically from your current or last position. It could include a profile and highlight relevant key skills and achievements before moving onto your employment history. With this format, you would show your employment history in reverse chronological order, starting with your current or last job.

- **Skills-based CV.** This format is particularly useful when you are considering a change in career direction and want to take the focus off your current or last job. With this format, the emphasis is on highlighting in more detail your key transferable skills and briefly summarising your employment history.

- **Academic CV.** CVs for academia may well be longer than the recommended 2 pages as they often list details of papers published as well as information relating to the candidate's area of expertise.

- **Single page CV.** This format is particularly useful for new entrants to the job market who have not yet built up extensive employment experience. While it is a useful format for networking by experienced professionals – particularly within financial services – if it is too short or concise, you could waste the opportunity to share some valuable information with the recruiter.

As you consider the best way to market yourself through your CV, ask yourself the following questions:

- What are the key skills and experience needed for the role I am applying for?

- What is the organisation looking for in hiring for this role?

- What are the issues that this company/sector/division faces?

- How relevant is my current/past experience to the sector or job role I am now targeting?

- What are my key skills for the job I'm looking for?

- Which transferable skills and attributes should I therefore highlight?

- Which of my achievements will best illustrate my skills?

- Which areas of my past experience are no longer relevant to the job I want?

- What else would this employer want to know about me?

What makes a CV effective, says Carol Hondonga of Rio Tinto, is when there is "a clear articulation of relevant career history, formal and relevant qualifications and the candidate has had exposure to other sectors and cultures."

By contrast, she adds, "For me, a poor application is when it looks like a cut and paste of job descriptions, when the candidate oversells by making it too detailed and including irrelevant information, and when I see inconsistent/ misrepresentation of information."

Example of CV Structure – Chronological CV

Full Name

Contact Details

Profile or Summary – this should align to the job you are targeting

Key Skills – highlight the skills you have that are needed for the role sought

Employment – include dates, company name, job title, brief summary of the role and highlight your key achievements

Educational and Professional Qualifications – include dates, educational institutions and key qualifications and certifications

Other Information – include nationality, interests, etc.

Referees – these can be stated as 'Available on request'

The following are a few tips to help you with your CV:

- Keep it professional by using a regular black font and checking for any spelling errors or omissions

- Customise your CV for each position, taking into account the requirements of the job

- Use strong verbs to convey your actions when describing job achievements (e.g. Acquired, Arranged, Conducted, Engineered, Established, Developed, Instigated, Managed, Strengthened, Planned)

- Don't leave any unexplained gaps between jobs

- Ensure that you use the right key words to allow for electronic scanning of your CV

- If in doubt about what to include, ask yourself whether it's relevant to your career objective or likely to be of interest to the organisation and the kind of impression you want people to have of you.

- Ask someone to review your CV – and preferably someone with experience in this area – to check on any spelling errors or omissions.

A great CV will focus on what matters most to the recruiter, and not on what matters to you, which means that the key word to keep in mind when writing your CV for the African job market is 'relevance'.

Are the skills you've highlighted in your CV the skills that are needed for the job you want? Is the context of your achievements clear to someone from another country? Are the achievements you've highlighted in your CV in line with the skills that you want to demonstrate?

The best way to writing a winning CV is to keep the job role and the organisation and its needs at the forefront of your thinking. Remember that selling involves showcasing benefits; as you select and construct the achievements you want to include in your CV, present them so that the benefits and the positive impact of the outcomes to the organisation are clear.

> *"What makes a CV attractive to me when I'm recruiting is when it is well laid out with a clear, structured outline of skills and achievements, and when the related experience is aligned to the vacancy announcement."*
>
> **HR Manager, International organisation, Zimbabwe**

Preparing for Interviews

Whether you have been selected for a job interview as a result of a formal recruitment process or through your network of contacts, once you are in front of a recruiter, actually getting that job will be down to only one person – you. An interview is your chance to bring to life the information on your CV and to give substance to the great referral you were given by your contact.

It's fair to say that there have been hundreds of books and articles written on how to prepare for and perform at interviews. Some recommend techniques ranging from practising assessment tests, setting up and practicing answers to difficult questions, and even learning deep-breathing techniques to counter nerves.

All of these are useful tips but it's important not to lose sight of the main goal. Because the simple reality is that an interview is where the employer is trying to establish three things: whether you have the skills needed for the job, the motivation required to put those skills to good use, and the personality and style of working that will fit in with the team and company.

Nevertheless, an interview is not a one-way street. It is also *your* opportunity to establish exactly what the job entails and that you can do it, whether the job is right for you in terms of your career strategy, and whether the people you will work with and the culture of the organisation make it a place where you can thrive and be successful. Furthermore, as you are seeking to work in a different country, it's also your chance to clarify what support will be available to help you make the transition.

How companies conduct job interviews can vary widely. Some may have recruiters based in your city or country who hire for their African markets, while others may want to conduct interviews by phone, Skype or in-country. Some companies will conduct an initial phone interview and, if you pass the first hurdle, will follow this up with a face to face interview.

In some cases, the first interview could be with a Human Resources or Recruitment executive who assesses whether to put you through for a subsequent meeting with the relevant department or operation. In other cases, companies prefer to have one of more senior managers interview prospective candidates first to assess their skills and ability to deliver on the requirements of the job. In the public and not-for-profit sectors, interviews are often conducted by a panel of people from within – and sometimes outside – the organisation.

Whether your interview is going to be held by phone or in person, preparing well is always going to be critical. Given that the organisation is trying to assess your skills, motivation and fit, prepare evidence to show that you have what it takes in all three areas.

Some typical lines of questioning that you can expect to be covered at interview include:

- Your technical skills relating to the job role

- Your knowledge of the country/company/job role

- Your motivation and your level of commitment to the move

- Your cultural awareness and ability to adapt to a new environment

- Your working style, team and communication skills

- Your management style (where relevant)

- Your career strategy/goals/expectations

- Your key strengths and areas of weakness

- Your flexibility and resilience

- Why they should hire you

Interview styles can range from informal discussions to structured interviews where each candidate is asked exactly the same questions and their responses are weighted according to their importance to the role.

The more in-depth your research about an organisation before an interview, the better you will be able to give the right responses. Finding out all you can about a company's culture and goals will help you position yourself as a strong candidate that not only has the technical ability, but also has the kind of qualities they look for when they recruit.

As interviews can vary so much, you might wonder how you can prepare adequately for the one you are invited to. No matter who is doing the hiring, there are some fundamental things to bear in mind if you want to win at job interviews.

- **Do your research.** Find out as much as you can about the company, the sector involved and the job role before you get to an interview. Try to research the LinkedIn profiles of the person or people interviewing you to learn more about them and their role in the business. Go through the CV or application you submitted and ensure that you are prepared to talk about anything on there.

- **Be specific.** Take ownership of your achievements by being as specific as possible, avoiding general statements and the use of 'we' instead of 'I'. Even if you are describing an achievement that involved a team of people, be clear about your role and how it contributed to the team's success.

- **Don't ramble.** Sometimes nerves can lead to too much talking – keep your answers focused on the specific question you were asked, not the general topic; the interviewer will ask you follow up questions if they want further details.

- **Tell your story.** Use specific stories from your employment or studies to illustrate your point; these are what will make you memorable. For example, if you are asked about your leadership skills, relate a specific instance that demonstrates how you lead others or manage yourself.

- **Know your strengths.** Think about the skills and competencies needed for the role and prepare your examples of when you have demonstrated these in the past. You should also be prepared to discuss your weaknesses i.e. areas where you are continuing to develop your skills, making sure that these are not areas that are critical to doing the job in question successfully.

- **Sell your soft skills.** Technical skills are only one part of what it takes to be successful in your career. How you use those skills will make all the difference, particularly as you are moving into a different cultural environment. Prepare evidence stories that back up your soft skills – skills such as teamwork, the ability to prioritise and plan work, show initiative, coach and lead others, work with people of different cultures, deal with stress, negotiate, influence and communicate with others.

- **Be the part.** Doing well at interview involves a lot of performing and getting your attitude, demeanour and body language right. Interviewers are trying to gauge how you will fit in with their organisation and they will need to like you before they put you forward. A key part of the interview process will be about your ability to look and sound the part and to bring good humour, positivity, enthusiasm and professionalism to the meeting, along with your skills and experience.

- **Know what's next.** Find out what the next stage of the interview process entails and the likely timescale involved. Some organisations can take some time to review interview results and get back to candidates. There may also be some formalities that need to be addressed before an offer can be made, such as an application for a work permit.

> *"What impresses me about candidates at interview is smart grooming, good verbal skills, natural body language, preparation for the interview, a genuine interest in the job and my company, good questioning, arriving on time, and the ability to demonstrate the required capability."*
>
> **Carol Hondonga, Rio Tinto**

An interview is also your opportunity to ask the questions that matter to you. Working in a different continent will involve a lot of change and a major commitment on your part. This means that you need to be really clear about the job on offer, the company in question, and how taking this role fits in with your career strategy. Remember that the questions you ask speak to your concerns and priorities, so be careful how you phrase your queries. Keep your focus on understanding the challenges and expectations of the role and the organisation.

As far as you can, avoid asking immediate questions about the salary and benefits on offer. These can be discussed at a later stage when the organisation has indicated that you are the right person for the job and for them.

Before the interview ends, try and uncover any concerns that the interviewer might have about your suitability for the job and do what you can to address these positively.

If the interview is taking place by phone or Skype:

- Make sure that your environment is clear of clutter and away from any potential interruptions or noise.

- If you are on webcam, keep your appearance and demeanour professional and have the interview in an appropriate room.

- Make a note of the person or people who are interviewing you and their role in the organisation so you can direct relevant questions to them.

- If you are not on webcam, keep a copy of the CV you submitted to that organisation in front of you so you can refer to the information if necessary, but avoid rustling papers.

- Listen carefully to the questions before responding and try not to interrupt the interviewer or speak over them.

- Have your own questions prepared ahead of time and note any others that come to mind during the interview.

- Agree next steps with the interviewer before completing the call.

> *"Particularly for those who come from the USA, the Ghana hiring system is very British and is more experience based than capability based. So one needs to be very specific on resumes or in interviews on how one's past experiences matter, and drawing very direct connections with the job or role of interest is key."*
>
> **Selorm Adadevoh, Ghana**

Recruiters are in the business of meeting people and forming judgements about them very quickly. A word that came up frequently when recruiters were asked about what made a candidate impressive at interview was 'confidence'.

For one particular HR Manager in Zimbabwe, this is a very important trait. "What impresses me are candidates who are confident and can show their relevant skills to the position being discussed; their ability to portray knowledge of the position and its expectations, a knowledge of the organisation and a potential and a willingness to learn", she says. "Professionals who want to work in Africa should be prepared to show what differentiates them from all the other candidates and to show that the skills they are bringing to the table will enhance the organisation's performance."

Conversely, the factors would make her reject a candidate include "complaints about their current employer, an inability to articulate how to handle the job requirements, being disrespectful, and candidates who come across as being interested only in what the organisation can provide and not what they can bring to the organisation."

Having a good network contact might have got you through the door, but it's important to keep them out of the interview. As Audrey Mensah of AMSCO admits, she is likely to reject a candidate who shows what she would consider "a lack of discretion, name dropping at every opportunity."

Successful job applicants are the ones who find solutions to the problems the employer is facing. Unsuccessful candidates are rejected either because they don't demonstrate to the employer how they will add value, or they don't know what they want to do and therefore can't articulate a compelling reason why they should be taken on.

For Keli Gadzekpo of Databank, a candidate who demonstrates a lack of knowledge about his industry or firm during a job interview is very likely to be turned down. What he finds impressive, he says, is "that they have researched my firm and what we do *and* relate it to how they can contribute to the firm."

Negotiating Compensation and Benefits

However much you want a job, it's unlikely that you will take it if the salary on offer is inadequate. During interviews and job discussions, the issue of compensation is quite often the elephant in the room; the thing that everyone knows is there, but no-one is ready to confront.

Knowing when to raise the salary question can be tricky; if you ask too early, you risk sounding as if it's the most important factor. If you leave it too late, you may have wasted time on a job that will not pay what you are looking for. When you also have to take account of the fact that you will be living in a different country, negotiating a good package becomes just as important as the job opportunity.

On the question of salaries in Africa, it's important to be realistic and not to assume that you can earn the equivalent of your current dollar or pound salary. One of the myths about a job in Africa centres on compensation, and as Elvina Quaison points out, "one of the big misconceptions people have about working in Africa is that they will fall into a lovely expat package!"

Your salary will reflect the demands of the market and the supply of talent available to organisations and you need to have an understanding of that market. Employers are only keen to recruit people from outside Africa if they feel that the experience they bring really adds value, Elvina says. "You are special if your skills are hard to come by. Otherwise you are competing with everyone else. There are an increasing number of skilled, internationally exposed, ambitious Ghanaians, and many employers are looking internally as much as possible."

Another point to bear in mind is that employers in Africa, particularly foreign based multinationals, are moving away from high value compensation packages. Where companies used to routinely offer the full expatriate package including a cost of living adjustment, housing, school fees, medical cover, home leave, domestic assistance and even support for the accompanying spouse, such benefits are increasingly falling by the wayside.

So while you may be dreaming of a high salary with expatriate benefits, your potential employer will have their own agenda and is more likely to be offering a fair salary; keeping a close eye on their costs, their local compensation structure, and their need to provide equity with their other employees and avoid unsustainable precedents.

As companies operating in Africa increasingly seek to attract overseas talent into specialist and management roles, their concern is to do it on a more cost-effective basis than the traditional expatriate model. A number of companies will offer a 'soft landing' to those joining them from abroad, which may include housing support or temporary accommodation, help to transport personal possessions and assistance with buying or leasing a car. Some will have laid down policies on what they offer to new hires and will have little room for manoeuvre, while others may be more willing to negotiate individual agreements to get the right person.

> *"Identify how much you want to earn, identify the cost of living and then decide on the country that can afford to pay you."*
>
> **AMSCO**

As with any negotiation scenario, negotiating your salary package requires you to be clear on your facts and to know what you are seeking to achieve. To do so, you need to research any data available and to use your network of contacts.

Research the cost of living in the country you have in mind and get a sense of what is needed to live the lifestyle that you are looking for. When reviewing what's on offer, don't just focus on the salary, but aim to clarify what the total package entails. Some companies pay a consolidated salary, while others may pay additional allowances or offer loans to help with big ticket items such as housing and transportation. Senior roles may include additional benefits such as a company car, subsidised or free fuel and utility allowances.

The cost of living will also vary from country to country, making it important that you understand the lifestyle your compensation will afford in that country, rather than how much you are being paid.

To be able to negotiate effectively, research the following:

- **Cost of living within your country of interest**. This should include costs of renting property (in some African countries, rent is payable at least a year in advance), utilities, transportation, food, clothing and socialising.

- **Local salary structure**. Research what comparable salaries look like for the level and type of job you are targeting through salary surveys, similar jobs posted online or advertised, and your network of contacts.

- **Company salary and compensation structure.** Through your recruitment consultant, headhunter or your contacts, find out what the company's compensation structure involves and the range of benefits that you will be entitled to.

- **Supply and demand for your skills.** The current demand for your skills will inform how much a company may be willing to pay. If there is a high demand for your skills set or the company is struggling to fill the role, this will impact on what they are prepared to pay for the right person.

Your research will help you determine your salary needs and figure out what your bottom line is in terms of salary and compensation. It will also give you an insight into what the company needs to consider and any constraints they have in ensuring that your package provides internal equity with their other employees.

A big myth about living in Africa, says Carol Hondonga of Rio Tinto, is the idea that someone coming from overseas will need a huge financial package. "One of the misconceptions that people can have about working in Africa is that they deserve to be paid a premium as they cannot have an acceptable standard of living on a local package."

This myth is one that Peter Ndegwa, a senior operations executive in Africa for Diageo, would like to dispel. "Expectations cannot always be met in terms of the lifestyle that people may seek, but this is often more about perception rather than reality," he says. "We have lots of European assignees who enjoy the experience and the quality of life and cost of living has become far better relative to Europe and the developed world."

Making a move to a different continent is a long-term career decision and in any negotiation you will need to give a little. Keep an open mind and be flexible when negotiating your package; if a company can't increase the base salary on offer, they may be able to offer other perks such as a more senior title, relocation support, or other useful benefits. Be prepared to be turned down if the company can't meet your terms and, if that is the case, keep your emotions in check.

While it's important to make sure that the package on offer is reflective of the role you will be taking on and the cost of living in that country, bear in mind that your starting salary is just one aspect of the opportunity. The type of work you will be exposed to and the learning opportunities it will bring should be a major factor in your thinking.

Remember also that reward does not only come in the form of money, but also with lifestyle. "It may sometimes not be as financially rewarding, but the pace of life may be ever so slightly better, reducing the many stresses people face in the West", says Audrey Mensah.

As you look at your career planning and evaluate these new opportunities, don't focus solely on the compensation. It could be that a modest salary along with a job that offers you stretch and a significant opportunity to grow your skills, could lead to a much more significant salary in the long-term.

Be careful how you come across in your negotiation. Audrey, for example, is wary of job applicants who put too great a focus on compensation. "I would reject a candidate when the only questions they come up with are to do with what they will get – salary and benefits – and not what they can contribute to their potential employer."

> *"Be realistic about your salary. You may need to take a salary cut, maybe give up on certain luxuries and trade these in for some 'inconveniences', but the latter also come with certain non-quantifiable benefits. This is a call that each individual will have to make for themselves!"*
>
> **Audrey Mensah, AMSCO**

Continue with your job search during the negotiating period and until an offer has been signed and sealed with your preferred organisation. If things don't work out, you will feel better knowing that you have other possible options open to you.

"Why O why did I ever leave my hobbit-hole?" said poor Mr. Baggins."

J.R.R. Tolkien, The Hobbit

Chapter 7

How Do I Handle the Change?

Moving your career to Africa can be a rewarding experience but, like any major change, it will bring with it many challenges. If you can handle the change and all its implications, you can have a successful transition; otherwise, you may well find yourself wondering why you ever made the move.

Managing Expectations of Africa

Moving to work in Africa is not the same as moving from London to Italy or from the USA to Germany. When it comes to Africa, we are talking about a very diverse continent with 54 countries that are at varying stages of economic and social development and you need to expect that there will be challenges.

Expectations are always hardest to manage when we don't know what to expect. This is another reason why researching the country and making a preliminary visit is so important. If you have had the chance to see the locality you will be working in and to meet some of your colleagues, you will be better prepared when you finally land.

While the degree of severity will vary from country to country, some of the most obvious challenges will include:

- Adjusting to local salaries and compensation packages

- Expensive housing and transportation

- Unreliable power and water supplies

- Poor transportation networks

- Language and cultural challenges

- Health and personal security

There are practical solutions to some of these issues which you can address during your preparation for departure or soon after you arrive. Others will be more a test of your ability to be flexible and to adapt to a new environment.

The best preparation for working in Africa, says Simi Belo, who moved to Nigeria from London, is in the mind. "You need to psychologically prepare for the fact that this is Africa," she says. "Things don't work and move the same way as overseas and some things will be different from what you are accustomed to. With this in mind, you can manage your expectations accordingly."

In dealing with these challenges, remember your motivation for making the move in the first place and be ready and willing to deal with these issues when they arise. Taking off your rose-coloured glasses and assessing the reality of the country you are living in allows you to be open to learning how to adapt to the change.

What are some of the things you can do to give you a better sense of what to expect when you move to work in Africa?

As you are making the move primarily to take up a job, your priority should be making sure that you are clear about your expectations of the job on offer, as well as the expectations of your new employers. The time to be clear about what the job will demand and what you are expected to deliver is *before* you take off, not afterwards.

This includes fully understanding the scope of the job and its objectives; how your performance will be assessed and managed, the level of support you can expect to have, and the likely development opportunities that will be available to you.

While many companies will have some form of onboarding or induction process for new employees, it's important to check whether there is such a policy in place at your new employers. If not, take the initiative to ask for an induction before you formally start work so that you can get an overview of the company and meet the key people you will be working with. Ask for an organisation structure chart and information about your team and colleagues.

"There will be a period of adjustment," says Belo. "Be aware that this is natural and normal; embrace it with a positive attitude and you will sail through."

Working in Africa can be tough, says Bernie Akporiaye. "The trick with managing your expectations is having clear goals for yourself. If you are able to do that, it will greatly help you through the inevitable difficult times by focusing you and enabling you to regard the tough situations as temporary and minor distractions in the general scheme of things."

> *"Expectations cannot always be met in terms of the lifestyle that people may seek, but this is often more about perception rather than reality. We have lots of European assignees who enjoy the experience and the quality of life and cost of living has become far better relative to Europe and the developed world."*
>
> **Peter Ndegwa, Diageo Africa**

For recruiters at African management services company, AMSCO, your ability to manage your expectations will reflect the extent of your commitment to making the move. "Realise that the fastest growing economies are in Africa and then decide if you want to be in the mix or not," they advise.

They encourage speaking to people to gain different insights into the real life difficulties that everyone has to manage, but also to take the time "to immerse yourself in the local culture to enable you to appreciate and enjoy the cultural surroundings."

One of the reasons often cited by people who want to work in Africa is the desire for more balance between their working and personal lives and to work in a less hectic environment.

Indeed, a key part of managing expectations for Africa is recognising that a change in pace will be inevitable.

As one HR Manager based in southern Africa says, "The pace in Africa is much slower than in the West, so one has to be prepared for that. Like any challenge, it's worth being committed to what you are doing and you will reap the rewards."

Much like anywhere else, your experience of working in an African country will depend to a large extent on the kind of company or organisation you choose to work for. While not every organisation operates at a high level of sophistication, you can increasingly expect to develop your career in some first-class organisations.

"Many companies are now desperate to get good talent, meaning that there are many more good career opportunities," says Peter Ndegwa, a senior operations executive in Africa for the global beverage corporation, Diageo. "Many companies in Africa are operating in the same way as overseas, and those abroad can make great steps in their careers here."

If you do choose to work in Africa, you will have to get yourself into the right frame of mind in order to be successful. For Elvina Quaison, what stood out when she made her move was the difference in the working environment. People's attitude to work is not the same as in the West, she says, and it is important to realise that social life and family responsibilities are taken very seriously and are key to how people operate, even at work.

"Don't take people's relaxed attitude as laziness or a lack of seriousness," she cautions. "Their attitude generally fits the environment. People work very hard but will also relax and enjoy themselves."

> *"Don't expect anything! Seriously, have no expectations. You will be disappointed if you go in with preconceptions. Go with the flow. As they say, 'there's no hurry in Africa.'"*
>
> **Ernestina Boadi**

Plugging into a Support System

Irrespective of your background or ethnicity, making a move to a different continent is a major decision. As with any significant change we want to make in our lives, having a good support system can make all the difference to the way we approach that decision and stay on track.

Your support system will include people that you can turn to for information, advice and inspiration and for keeping you motivated when your spirits are flagging or you are feeling overwhelmed. However, your supporters can also come in the form of those who offer words of caution and who can help you to be sure that before you set off on an adventure, you have thought it through properly and are really prepared for what lies ahead.

Recognise who makes up your personal ecosystem of support and the ways in which they can help you explore your interest and motivation for working in Africa and advise and guide you as you make the move.

> *"It is difficult adapting to a new environment and trying to make your professional and personal life function positively, but I keep on, and I look to friends and family for support."*
>
> **Elvina Quaison**

From the very start of your thought process about making this journey, seek out advisers who know you and who can give you honest and objective feedback about whether you have the right skills and attitude to be successful in a career in Africa.

Although they may not know much about the countries or even the job opportunities you are considering, ask them if you are the kind of person that has an open mind, a flexible disposition, the ability to get on with people of different backgrounds and cultures, and are able to adapt to new ways of doing things. These traits, as much as your technical skills, will be critical to your ability to do well with your career in Africa.

A key part of your support system will be those who encourage you to explore your motivations for making the move and why you think this move will bring you the changes you want to make in your life.

Another element will be those who have direct knowledge of working in Africa or who can direct you to people within their network, both within and outside Africa, who can help with your planning. Once you reach out for help and advice, you could be surprised at how many people will respond.

Make a list of the type of support you need and the people who can help you in the ways you need. Your personal ecosystem of support should include a variety of people, such as:

- People who will help me to think about my motivation for working in Africa and my aspirations

- People who will help me explore the skills and competencies that I should focus on when selling myself

- People who know, or can connect me to, others in their network who know the realities of working in Africa

- People who know my personality and can help me understand whether this is the right path for me

- People who will encourage and cheer me on when I'm feeling discouraged

- People who can help or coach me to develop a strategy for making the move and to get myself in front of the right employers

- People who will keep me on track when I'm getting confused or losing focus

- People who can advise me about what I need to have in place before I leave and when I arrive in Africa

- People who can help me settle in and adjust to a new job and to living in a new country

Once you are clear about what you need, it is easier to identify who to turn to and the kind of support or advice that you would like from them or from their contacts.

Joining networks and communities of like-minded people and other professionals will also give you an invaluable support system. These can be associations and networks of professionals that hold actual events and activities, or virtual networks and online communities. On LinkedIn, for example, there are thousands of online groups that you can join and where you can interact with other people from your profession or area of expertise, as well as people living and working in the country you plan to move to.

Both before and after your move, developing strong relationships will be a valuable factor in helping you manage your expectations of working in Africa, says Elvina Quaison. "Things do not work as quickly or smoothly as you may expect or hope and relationship building with everyone is key to getting things done as you would like."

> *"My business was an idea which I had developed from my last job role in the UK. Through networks and trial and error, I am still here."*
>
> **Elvina Quaison, Ghana**

Dealing with Culture Shock

We are all products of our cultural upbringing and the values, assumptions and ways of seeing the world that were instilled in us from our earliest years. Our culture influences us to such an extent that we act upon it instinctively; from the way we speak to our family members to the way we behave with our colleagues and managers.

We can be surprisingly unaware of how deep our own cultural norms are until we find ourselves in a completely new environment. Suddenly, all the things we would usually take for granted can appear alien and even unwelcome. The way we think, behave, speak, eat and even what we find funny may no longer be what is acceptable, and we can truly feel like a stranger in a foreign land.

Even for those who originate from Africa, returning to work in the continent can be a challenge. Expectations based on one's previous experience of living, or even working, in a country that one thinks of as home, can lead to frustration and a sense of confusion because things change and you have changed.

For Africans who left the continent to live and work abroad, trying to reintegrate into an environment that should be familiar but may no longer feel so, can be difficult. Peter Ndegwa of Diageo points out that "People and companies have moved on and Africans in the diaspora at times do feel challenged in coming back and fitting in."

Paul Kasimu, another senior executive with Diageo, acknowledges that time spent away from Africa can make reintegration difficult for professionals of African origin.

"What I have seen is that people come back as completely different people from when they left," he says. "Returning from the diaspora often leads to culture shock as people come and find a totally different world from what they knew and also from where they are coming from. This change is also evident in our ways of working and even how to act."

If you don't know Africa, you will have fewer expectations of what life will be like and how things used to be and, therefore, you may well be better prepared to embrace a change in culture and style of work. If Africa is new to you, while you will notice some similarities with your own country of origin, you will almost certainly find many differences in culture and behaviour.

It is easier to appreciate the obvious differences in cultures such as language, food, style of dress and music. We can see and hear these differences and can react to them appropriately. What is harder to understand are the hidden aspects of a different culture – the invisible rules that define each society, making it harder to avoid the conflicts that arise when we try to interpret one culture through another set of cultural rules and norms.

Although you have been hired for your skills and experience, if you can focus on trying to understand your new environment first, it will help you to fulfil your role more effectively.

As Selorm Adadevoh, a senior business development professional who moved from the United States to Ghana says, "Working on being accepted early is a much better route to being effective than coming in and proving all things wrong or inferior."

While it is impossible to generalise about a continent as diverse as Africa, it's probably fair to say that some attitudes are fairly widespread among Africans. For example, you are likely to notice a greater importance placed upon family; not only the immediate nuclear family, but the extended family. This attitude impacts the workplace with practices such as offering financial contributions for significant family-related events, or sending delegations of staff to funerals when work colleagues or important clients suffer bereavements in their families.

You may also find that there can be more formality in the workplace than in the West, where first names are used much more freely when addressing senior management. In contrast with the rather more egalitarian workplaces typical in the UK or the USA, companies in Africa can appear more hierarchical and status conscious.

> *"It is key to come in with an open mind. While you may be experienced, there is still a lot about the culture, how businesses operate and the consumer behaviour that needs to be learned. It's a 2-way learning street and while one may bring a lot to the table, without learning the system well and understanding how and why things are done in the way they are, one's decisions may be very flawed."'*
>
> **Selorm Adadevoh, Ghana**

Social relationships are based on networks of connections created through families, schools, work, churches, and associations and they offer informal sources of advice and mutual support. These networks are actively used to help provide information, source contacts and navigate bureaucracy.

A well-known cultural trait that is widespread in Africa is the generally relaxed attitude towards time keeping. While it can be frustrating to deal with meetings that do not start on time or appointments that are made against very fluid timeframes, it is important to be aware that this is an ingrained attitude in many societies. Be prepared for what you consider to be urgent to be perceived quite differently by others, and build this into your planning.

Language forms a major part of communication and although you may be speaking in English, French or Portuguese when you work in Africa, you should be mindful that words may be interpreted differently, depending on the culture you are operating in. Humour based on sarcasm or insults offered in fun, for example, may not be appreciated in the same way as in the West, and could cause deep offence. You should also tread cautiously and respectfully when discussing topics that excite deep passions across the continent, such as politics, religion and sport.

If you have no past experience of living in an African country and therefore do not have an understanding of these norms, falling in line can be a major test of your patience and your ability to adapt.

Even if you are familiar with the country you will be working in, don't expect to immediately fit into your new organisation. Any new job requires a period of adjustment; anticipate this so that you are not disheartened as you try and navigate your new environment.

It is a lesson that Elvina Quaison learned after moving to Ghana. "Prepare yourself for a different mindset when it comes to work," she cautions. "What is common sense to you will not be the same in Africa, as 'common sense' is derived from cultural, environmental and social norms. Those in Africa will be different to those elsewhere."

One of the benefits of moving your career into Africa is the opportunity to develop your ability to work with and manage across diverse cultures, a skill that is increasingly important in businesses and for those working in global companies.

Your ability to motivate and manage those who report to you will hinge on how well you adapt to the culture you will be working in. Effective leaders need to have cultural agility and be able to adapt their own cultural norms to those that are dominant where they are working. Working overseas will not automatically make you culturally agile; it is a skill you will need to develop by being conscious of your own emotions, norms and biases and being ready to change your mindset and be open to different ways of seeing a situation.

Travel really does broaden the mind and it also allows you to question your own assumptions and ways of doing things. What works well in the environment you came from may prove to be inappropriate to your new location. By first learning how things work in a new country, you will be able to adjust your own behaviour accordingly.

"It's preferable for a company to hire someone that has a less impressive track record of achievements, but who can adapt quickly to the environment and deliver in the job."

AMSCO

Changing Mindset

For many of us, change sounds like an exciting idea and one that offers new possibilities. However, once we are placed in a situation of change, we can often find ourselves becoming resistant to new concepts, and seeing them as threatening our norms and values and our personal sense of stability.

However irrational it may be, we begin to question why others can't be more like us and we attempt to change our environment rather than ourselves, feeling despondent when, of course, we don't succeed.

If you intend to make a move to work in Africa, you need to accept that you are the one moving to a foreign location and that if anyone needs to adapt in order to survive, it will have to be you.

Many of those interviewed for this book stressed the importance of changing mindset when you move to Africa. Frustration management is critical, warns Selorm Adadevoh.

"Be ready to take a chill pill – you will likely be frustrated several times but don't allow yourself to keep comparing things to the US or the UK or wherever you came from. It's a bit unfair to the locals and it won't exactly help move things forward. The 'In the US, things work better' speech is not very welcome," he says.

Trying to introduce change needs to be done in a measured and considered way, he advises. "In my experience, the best way to impact change is to explain the better option and what the benefits of the alternative options are within the context of the situation and that should be it. No reference needs to be made to the US or UK or another country. Simply make the point instead!"

> *"Go with an open mind and a willingness to learn. Once you have an idea of how things work, you can combine your working style with that of the organisation so that you work in harmony with each other, not in conflict. Your way is not necessarily the better way; it's just your way."*
>
> **Elvina Quaison**

Making the decision to stay is important if you are to realise the benefits of the decision to move in the first place. While she enjoys the friendly environment and the "buzz of opportunity and possibility", living in Africa is not always easy, says Elvina Quaison.

"Infrastructural problems, poor health care, poor road safety and indiscipline of drivers, cultural differences, and differences in mindset all contribute their challenges," she admits. "It is generally the little things that are continuous that will eventually wear you out and make you want to leave. Patience and finding ways to overcome the irritations are your only way forward if you are determined to stay."

However personally inconvenient it may prove, things are what they are, says Ernestina Boadi, now living and working in Ghana. "After enjoying first world public transport that is accessible, affordable and works, if you don't have a car or driver here, it's tough as you have to find your way around."

Patience is a word often touted by those questioned about their move to Africa. "You have to learn patience if you want to succeed," admits Boadi. "You have to accept that there will be different standards and approaches." This view was endorsed by one HR Manager in southern Africa who cautioned that "one needs to give it enough time to see the benefits."

You really need to prepare for working in Africa, says Carol Hondonga of Rio Tinto. "Be flexible and prepared to adapt to living in a developing country with its challenges. Re-orient yourself with the culture and seek to integrate and not appear as being superior."

On the issue of superiority, Audrey Mensah of AMSCO warns against making assumptions. "If you do come to Africa, do not feel that you are superior to the locally trained personnel; some may be a lot more skilled and experienced than you."

Working in Africa will give you the opportunity to learn not only new skills but also new insights about yourself, says Ernestina Boadi. "I've learned that I'm a lot stronger, more patient and more tolerant than I thought I was. In the West you have more control over things and can be more organised. Now I can sit and wait for people to get to a meeting, even when they are very late, and not show any signs of urgency about the time or get so easily frustrated."

> *"The purpose of life is to live it, to taste experience to the utmost, to reach out eagerly and without fear for newer and richer experience."*
>
> **Eleanor Roosevelt**

Being successful in your role in Africa will require a change of mindset. Moving locations is a change that will require *you* to change, not the country you are going to. As you plan to set off on your adventure, make it one that you will enjoy by being open to everything that might come your way.

"Toto, I have a feeling we're not in Kansas anymore."

Dorothy, The Wizard of Oz

Chapter 8

How Do I Plan my Move?

If you fail to plan your departure properly, you will almost certainly be planning to fail. A poorly planned relocation process can make an already difficult situation highly stressful and set you off on your adventure on a sour note.

As Elvina Quaison points out, "The dream of moving 'home' is great; the reality needs planning, resilience and a budget."

If you are relocating with your family, you will have some additional challenges to navigate. Making a career move to a new continent will not affect you alone, making it important that you have open and honest discussions about a move with all concerned before taking any decisions.

Audrey Mensah of AMSCO advises that "if you are moving with family, make sure that you discuss it with your spouse and sensitize them."

The majority of international assignments that fail are the result of dissatisfaction by the spouse and/or other family members. So getting everyone involved onside and excited about your decision to move will be vital if you are to be successful.

Factor in the cost of moving your family, she warns. "If you have children, identify schools, check the availability and time of class intake, check the fees and make sure you can afford it if your new employer is not paying!"

Your impending move will involve putting a number of things in place and the process can sometimes seem overwhelming. Think about it as a project and approach the move in a disciplined way, keeping track of where you are and what needs to be done in the time that you have.

As with any project, you need to be clear about your budget. Go through all the likely costs that will arise and be sure that you are financially ready to make the move. Plan for the unexpected and have money available for contingencies and emergencies, particularly if you will have ongoing commitments in your home country after you move.

If your move to Africa is an international move within your company, your employer is likely to have policies that include providing relocation assistance for you and your family. However, there are also experienced relocation companies that offer a full package of support for those entering a new location and you can search for these or use your network of contacts to identify someone on the ground that can help you with the settling in process.

Before Departure

There are a number of critical issues that you should address as part of your relocation planning.

Immigration, Visas & Work Permits

Unless you are being employed by a company that is organising your visa (and visas for your family), you will need to check on the immigration requirements to work in the country of your choice and the time it takes to process applications. This information is normally available from the relevant Embassies, High Commissions and Consular offices.

If you hold nationality of the African country you are moving to and your spouse or dependents do not, you should also check on the immigration requirements for them and any restrictions – such as the right of your spouse to work – that may be imposed on them.

You will have to pay fees for visas and permits and you should expect to be asked to produce documents such as passports (check they are valid and renew any that are due to expire), marriage certificates, birth certificates, vaccination and medical certificates. For certain countries, you may also need to produce offer letters of employment and educational certificates as evidence of a job and your suitability for the role.

If you are not a citizen of the country you currently reside in, you should check on any restrictions or requirements needed to retain your residency status if you leave to work overseas. Seek advice from qualified professionals on your continued residency rights – and that of any family members or dependents – once you have left your country of residence.

Health & Medical

Staying healthy is critical if you are to enjoy your adventure and this is one of the key issues to address. Research the climate and the likely health concerns in that country. Vaccinations can offer protection against some of the diseases prevalent in Africa, while you can help safeguard yourself against others by taking the proper precautions.

Seek specialist advice from a travel clinic or doctor and plan your vaccinations and immunisations well in advance of travel as some vaccinations are administered over a period of weeks and not just as one shot. For some African countries, Cholera and Yellow Fever vaccinations are mandatory to gain entry. You should also consider being vaccinated against specific diseases as a matter of course. Information about the immunisations recommended or required can be obtained from your doctor or a travel clinic.

While your new company may offer local medical cover, you should also investigate international medical insurance plans that offer a range of benefits including medical evacuation to your home country in an emergency, or to the nearest country offering equivalent care.

Transportation of Personal Belongings

Along with the joy of making a new start will also be the headache of packing up your home and possessions, and anxiety about getting the things you need safely to your new location. Make your move a little smoother by getting organised and finding a trustworthy removals or shipping company to transport your belongings.

Use lists and reminders to help you stay on top of all that needs to be done. Leave yourself plenty of time to pack so you can organise all of your belongings logically. Pack your belongings into categories and label them – it will save you hours when you arrive at your new home.

If you are able to visit the country ahead of your move, research the area you are moving to and gather as much information as you can and, if possible, speak to people who live or have lived in that area.

Verify the documents needed to both export your goods from the country you are leaving and import them to your destination and any duties or taxes that you may have to pay.

Make sure to keep important papers with you and not in the goods being shipped. This includes birth certificates, marriage licenses, stock certificates, divorce decrees, custody papers, passports, social security cards, etc. You should also keep handy school records that you may need to register your children in new schools and any documents that would be hard to replace.

Housing

You will need to deal with making arrangements for your home as well as plan where you will be staying when you have relocated.

Take professional advice on renting or selling your home and any implications this may have on your tax and residency status. Make arrangements to re-direct mail to an alternative address and notify your bank of your change of address. You should also contact and cancel utility services and internet and mobile phone providers.

Personal Finances

Changing residence may also impact how you report and/ or pay taxes in both your home and host countries and on your rights to re-enter your host country once you have left. You should notify the relevant tax and social security authorities and make decisions on personal financial products such as your pension, life assurance and other policies. Make sure to keep enough funds in the right currency to continue to service any ongoing payments you need to make when you move, such as a mortgage.

Ask about transferring money and if there are any restrictions in taking money out of the country you are moving to, should you decide to return home or move elsewhere.

Tax and finance experts can help you plan these important issues before you leave.

> *"Educate the people you are leaving behind and reassure them, as their worrying becomes your worrying. Send pictures and tell them to visit."*
>
> AMSCO

After Arrival

In an ideal world, you will have made at least one visit to your chosen country prior to relocating and will know what to expect.

If not, research and find out the facts about life in the country of your choice. Don't rely solely on anecdotal information from friends or even relations; different people have different opinions, and what might be the 'perfect location to live in' or the 'best school' may be very different from what you had in mind! Get the facts about your destination and take nothing for granted.

Immediately you arrive, sorting out your accommodation, a bank account, a doctor, schools and a car will be among your immediate priorities. You will also need to register your phone to a network, arrange any driving licenses or permits and car insurance, and possibly hire domestic staff. Your new company, as well as your network of contacts, will be invaluable in helping you navigate your way through the processes in the early weeks.

Many companies will provide or pay for temporary accommodation while you find your feet; while others may have a guest house or company house that you can make use of.

Think carefully about the location of your property. Where will you be working? What schools are your children likely to attend? Do you want to be in town or live further out? Find out about crime in the area and issues such as likely traffic congestion before making a decision. In recent years, property developments and private estates have sprung up in many countries and have become very popular as they often offer security and impose strict maintenance regulations.

In some countries, rent is paid in advance for periods of up to a year or even longer. Your pre-departure research will have given you the information you need to make an informed choice and, as credit is much harder to access in Africa, companies are often able to offer assistance in the form of housing loans or rent advances, or guarantee bank loans that you take out for this purpose.

It will take some time to settle in and make the adjustment to living in a different country. If you have children, you will need to enrol them into a new school and finding one that uses a similar curriculum will help make their transition smoother. Choosing a school with an education system affiliated to your home country will also make it easier for your children to re-enter your home education system if you decide to leave Africa while they are still at school.

Additionally, their education and qualifications obtained overseas will be more likely to be recognised by your home country colleges and universities.

Establish if you need to register with any authorities and make a point of registering with your local Embassy or High Commission. This will help your government to keep in touch with you if you get into difficulties, or in case of any emergencies.

Take your personal safety and security seriously to avoid any problems; seek advice on where it is safe to travel and socialise, and take common sense precautions to ensure that you enjoy your adventure.

It will also take some time for your body to acclimatise to your new environment and you will need to pay careful attention to your diet and food hygiene when you arrive. Seek out advice and information to help you manage the risks. If you have specific health issues, identify clinics that can deal with your condition and that cater to international patients.

Depending on your location, you may have to deal with unreliable infrastructure and erratic supplies of utilities such as water and electricity. The impact of this can be mitigated to some extent by investing in equipment such as generators and water tanks, but this is a feature of life in many parts of Africa that you have to accept.

> *"Keep in mind that everyone goes through a lot of common challenges and ongoing frustrations. Patience is required all along the way."*
>
> AMSCO

Settling into Work

As you prepare to start your new job, remind yourself that it will take time to adjust to the people, the systems and the working culture. Leaving behind friends and family is not an easy thing to do and to make the sacrifice worthwhile you need to be mentally tough and prepared for challenges.

If you are rejoining friends and family and returning to your country of origin in Africa, the benefits will help you overcome the challenges. As Simi Belo admits, "What makes returning worthwhile is the people. It's all about family; none of us has returned for the infrastructure!"

Yet, even if you originate from Africa, making the transition to working within Africa after a long period of time abroad is not always an easy exercise. Simi admits that she has learned "professionally and personally to pick my battles" and to be selective about what she allows to frustrate her.

"It is actually quite tough to reintegrate," says Selorm Adadevoh, a senior manager within the Telecoms sector who returned to his native Ghana after a number of years living and working in the United States. "At times, I wonder if I ever will! But it is important to integrate more with the true locals to continue to understand how things work. Returnees tend to flock together and, while it is okay at first, it is a real barrier to properly immersing oneself back into the local culture. My message is to think about this and decide where you want to play."

This advice is echoed by AMSCO, who advise that you must "understand the local context as this will lead to a successful transition and integration."

So while it may be tempting to find and stick with people from your own community who can provide you with the familiarity of your culture and a network of support, aim to integrate into your host country as soon as you arrive. You will be able to learn more about the country and fit in quicker if you broaden your circle of friends.

You will benefit from reading up on the differences between your own culture and that of your new destination to help you avoid cultural misunderstandings. You can also integrate more quickly into your new life and work culture by:

- Understanding the impact of cultural differences on work performance and relationships and accepting that this may be very different to what you know.

- Making an effort to develop empathy with your colleagues and partners from other cultural backgrounds

- Focusing on developing communication and management strategies that work in a multi-cultural environment

- Learning the language or a few key phrases to help earn you some goodwill and open the door to new relationships

- Engaging with people passively in a listening/learning mode to begin with; you can be more active in your contributions once you are clear about what is needed and what is appropriate to where you are

- Not limiting your circle to other 'expats' only and learning to integrate so you can develop a strong local network of people to support and guide you through tough times

- Taking an interest in the country and joining a local club or society to make new contacts and expand your network.

- Travelling around the country to learn more about its history and culture and interacting with the local population.

With the technology now available, it is much easier to stay in touch with friends and family at home. If you are in Africa on a fixed-term assignment, make the effort to also keep in touch with your contacts at your company's headquarters and continue to build a network that will keep you in mind for future international opportunities.

> *"Coming to Ghana has indeed been very challenging but, so far, very rewarding."*
>
> **Selorm Adadevoh**

Establish with your managers what your priorities should be and set expectations accordingly. You should also try to understand how your success will be measured and, if there is a performance management system, how it operates in practice. Consider setting yourself some personal and work goals to work towards and to help you measure how effective you are being. In today's competitive world of work, it is a myth that expectations are not as high as in the West and that one can get away with mediocre performance at work.

Even where you do find that, in some circumstances, standards vary from what you are used to, Bernie Akporiaye advises that you should "never lower yours, because that's your unique selling point."

This advice is echoed by Ernestina Boadi who finds that standards can vary widely even within organisations. "If you don't find a way to focus on what you are doing and ignore the frustrations that can arise from trying to bring everyone up to your standards, you won't survive," she says.

First impressions are crucial and as you navigate your new workplace, keep in mind how you want to be perceived, taking note of the dress code even if it is not formally stated as such. Actively build good work relationships, not only with the people you will work with regularly, but also with those in other departments and participate in social and cultural events and team activities. Seek out people who can act as supporters and mentors for you as you make the transition.

Over time, you will become more familiar with your new role, the company and your colleagues. While conflict is inevitable in any workplace, it's particularly important that you deal with disagreements in the right way when you are working in a new environment.

When conflicts arise, remain calm, tread carefully and communicate respectfully with those around you. Africans are traditionally inclined to show respect to their elders and seniors and do not react well to younger people behaving in an overly authoritative manner towards them. If you are ready to listen and to deal sensitively with those around you, you will be able to defuse conflicts far more effectively.

You will find that there are many other highly educated and well-travelled people wherever you go, and a diplomatic approach to bringing new ideas into your workplace will be critical. Introduce new approaches where they are welcome and when you understand how things are done. As Carol Hondonga of Rio Tinto advises, "Have a genuine passion and partnership mentality in working with the locals. Learning and sharing is a two-way process."

Use your skills and experience not to try to revolutionise the business, but to enhance your contribution to your new employer and to your own development. The right way to approach working in Africa, says a senior HR manager based in Zimbabwe, is to have "a good work ethic, be positive, be organised and be flexible."

If you approach it in the right way and with the right spirit, working in Africa can be a fantastic adventure, says Audrey Mensah. "Many others have come to work in Africa, are making an honest living and have been successful. So it is possible for you too!"

> *"Life is either a daring adventure, or nothing."*

Hellen Keller

Conclusion

Moving your career to an emerging region such as Africa will bring you a number of tangible and intangible benefits. You will experience a lot of learning and are likely to have more responsibilities in a shorter time period than in other parts of the word, accelerating the progress of your career. You will gain a lot, both personally and professionally, and almost certainly find it a highly rewarding experience.

The final question to ask yourself is when is the right time to make your move to Africa? Only you can decide this, based on your personal circumstances.

It may be that family ties and responsibilities such as school-age children make an immediate move impractical; or that financial obligations such as mortgages, loans, health considerations and other constraints make relocation in the short or even medium term unlikely.

If you are young and of African origin, one consideration will be whether you can benefit from gaining more international work experience before returning home. For those on particular career tracks, gaining international experience is increasingly becoming a prerequisite for future success in their countries of origin in Africa.

On the other hand, you may feel that you would like to start your career in Africa and perhaps look at gaining overseas experience at a later stage. Alternatively, you may, for instance, want to work in Africa as a transition to starting a business or some form of self-employment.

Whatever you decide about the timing of your adventure into Africa, plan your move carefully to get the best of the experience.

As you consider what Africa holds for you, don't be put off by the negative myths and stereotypes, but instead consider the facts. The continent holds 1 billion people, which is 15% of the world's population. Unlike the pictures often shown in the media, nearly half its people live in cities. Economic growth on the continent has stayed well above the global average since 2000, and is projected to continue. Today, out of the 54 countries on the African continent, only 8 are dealing with conflicts, as compared to 30 countries back in 1990.

In the same way as the increasing numbers of businesses moving into and expanding across Africa are doing, you can also take advantage of the opportunities on the continent today.

You may be in a comfortable place in your career, feeling secure and not inclined to take a risk. But what might you be missing in terms of your career growth? And might you be even more at risk if you play it safe and don't take the opportunity to broaden your horizons, deepen your experience and stretch yourself? How else might you build your confidence to take on new projects and your ability to lead across different cultures?

As John A Shedd says in '*Salt from My Attic*', "A ship in harbour is safe, but that is not what ships are built for."

Staying in your comfort zone is not what you were built to do. Africa is not for the faint-hearted, but for those who are prepared to invest time to plan and energy to understand its people and customs, it can be the most exciting and rewarding place to work.

The most important thing to remember about the African job market is that the greatest challenge that businesses in Africa face today is the ability to attract the level and quality of talent to meet their needs. But finding a job takes planning and persistence. Using a variety of approaches will improve your odds of finding the right job with the right employer.

As Ugandan consultant Collison Lore advises, "Using a combination of methods is essential for a successful job search in an African country. It is essential to develop a strategy that works best for the occupations you are seeking, while remembering to adapt it to local conditions. Ask questions like: how did others in the same or similar fields find their jobs? Was it through networking, a headhunter, a newspaper advertisement, a posting on a web site or with a government agency?

"Answers to these questions may offer crucial leads to the success of your job search. Always remember that, just as in more developed markets, one size does not fit all, so develop a job search campaign that targets your specific career goals. Research, however, is the number one prospecting method that is not adequately utilised by job seekers who may assume rightly or wrongly that their international qualifications, experience and exposure are enough."

To work successfully in Africa, you have to be able to deal with the challenges. You need to have high levels of energy, adaptability, cultural sensitivity and resilience. You will be in a new country, a new home, hearing different languages, working with different teams, fitting in with new people, understanding new clients and markets, and working at a different pace. It's a lot to take in.

To be successful, you need to be flexible, to develop your listening skills, and demonstrate a willingness to learn.

Will it be easy? Probably not. But you will never know unless you try. "If you don't take risks, you'll have a wasted soul," says the actress Drew Barrymore. Or, as Nita Morgan puts it more prosaically, "Make everything an adventure. Otherwise, it will suck."

So plan to mitigate the risks, but make the journey. Enjoy the journey. Have your adventure. And if it's home you're returning to, bring back the best of what you learned while you were gone.

I encourage you to use all the information in this book to reflect and be courageous about taking action. If moving your career to Africa is what you want, be persistent and the doors will eventually open for you.

Now, are you ready for the adventure that is Africa?

"*Why do you go away? So that you can come back. So that you can see the place you came from with new eyes and extra colours. And the people there see you differently, too. Coming back to where you started is not the same as never leaving.*"

Terry Pratchett, A Hat Full of Sky

To Help You Get Started…

Useful Resources

ReConnect Africa (www.ReConnectAfrica.com)

A careers, business and news website and bi-monthly magazine for professionals of African origin around the world. ReConnect Africa provides a wealth of information, including listings of recruiters in Africa, employers in Africa, African professional networks, African media and a jobs portal. The bi-monthly magazine features business and careers articles, news, an events diary, and interviews with employers, entrepreneurs and African professionals around the world.

ICT Africa (www.ictafrica.info/searchJob.php)

A portal allowing companies, organisations, government departments and entrepreneurs to share ICT opportunities with African professionals.

Top Employers (www.top-employers.com)

A listing of companies independently certified by the Top Employers Institute as Top Employers in selected African countries.

CultureCrossing.Net (www.culturecrossing.net)

A database of cross-cultural information about every country in the world and allows people from all walks of life to share essential tips with each other. Helps travellers, business people and students to find information on 200+ countries, ask experts and access global resources on cross-cultural exploration.

World Business Culture (www.worldbusinessculture.com)

Culture-focused country profiles with information on a range of topics compiled by some of the world's leading experts on global business culture.

Foreign & Commonwealth Office (www.fco.gov.uk)

The site has a useful search tool to access the London Diplomatic List which contains the addresses and contact details of all Embassies, High Commissions and Consulates.

SouthAfrica.Info (www.southafrica.info)

Brand South Africa's information gateway to South Africa with information about the country, travelling to and doing business in South Africa.

Driving Abroad (www.drivingabroad.co.uk)

Provides advice, equipment and information to help make sure you are prepared for foreign driving laws and emergency situations.

World Weather Information Service
(www.worldweather.org)

Global web site with weather observations, weather forecasts and climatological information supplied by National Meteorological & Hydrological Services (NMHSs) worldwide.

Expat Info Desk (www.expatinfodesk.com)

Expat Info Desk is an online resource specializing in international relocation guide services.

Teach Yourself (www.teachyourself.co.uk)

Teach yourself courses in over 60 languages.

Organisations

AMSCO (www.amsco.org)

AMSCO's primary objective is to assist African companies by providing qualified, experienced, hands-on, professional management and related services to selected private companies and commercially operated public enterprises.

Homecoming Revolution: The one-stop platform that brings home African Diaspora Professionals (www. homecomingrevolution.com)

Established in South Africa in 2003, Homecoming Revolution is the one-stop platform that showcases careers, properties, schools, relocation services, investments and entrepreneurial opportunities in South Africa, Nigeria, Kenya, Uganda and Ghana. Activities include global expos, local networking meetings, an interactive website, a job portal, regular newsletters and tailored recruitment services.

InterHealth Worldwide (www.interhealthworldwide.org/)

A UK-based international health charity preparing, sustaining and supporting the health and wellbeing of individuals working around the world.

Masta Travel (www.masta-travel-health.com)

Travel health information with free travel briefs.

Council of British International Schools (COBIS) (www.cobis.org.uk)

Association providing information about British International Schools around the world.

African Foundation for Development (AFFORD) (www.afford-uk.org)

Provides expertise and useful information about developments, projects and activities relating to Africans in the diaspora.

*We salute **Madiba**, the inspiration of our nation.*

South Africa

Inspiring new ways

Nigerian Breweries Plc
RC: 613

FIND YOUR PLACE IN THE HOME OF GREAT BRANDS

As part of our mission *"To be the leading beverage company in Nigeria, marketing high quality brands to deliver superior customer satisfaction in an environmentally friendly way"*, we are constantly on the look-out for people who can rise to the challenges of the company today, and yet, are flexible enough to dream and grow with us as we create the brewing industry of tomorrow.

Winning with Nigeria

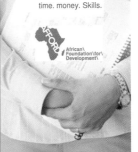

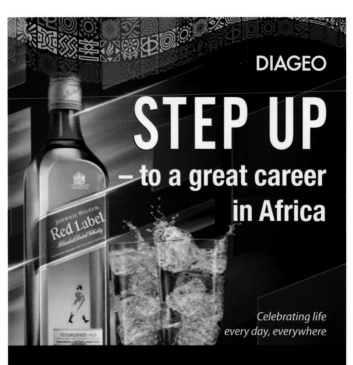

What role could you play in Africa's leading independent Oil company?

Tullow Oil plc is Africa's leading independent oil company. Our exploration-led growth strategy is focused on light oil in Africa and the Atlantic Margins. We are a highly successful explorer opening four new oil basins in Africa and South America in the last seven years.

We are looking for people in Kenya, Mauritania, Ghana and Uganda with excellent commercial and technical skills, with entrepreneurial flair.

Visit our website to find out more about our business, our values and our opportunities.

www.tullowoil.com/careers